Mathmatters

This book is part of the Goodyear Series in Education, Theodore W. Hipple, University of Florida, Editor

OTHER GOODYEAR BOOKS IN SCIENCE, MATH, & SOCIAL STUDIES

THE CHALLENGE OF TEACHING SOCIAL STUDIES IN THE ELEMENTARY SCHOOL
Dorothy J. Skeel

DR. JIM'S ELEMENTARY MATH PRESCRIPTIONS   *Activities—Aids—Games to Help Children Learn Elementary Mathematics*
James L. Overholt

THE EARTHPEOPLE ACTIVITY BOOK   *People, Places, Pleasures, and Other Delights*
Joe Abruscato and Jack Hassard

ECONOMY SIZE   *From Barter to Business With Ideas and Activities*
Carol Katzman and Joyce King

LEARNING TO THINK AND CHOOSE   *Decision-Making Episodes for the Middle Grades*
J. Doyle Casteel

LOVING AND BEYOND   *Science Teaching for the Humanistic Classroom*
Joe Abruscato and Jack Hassard

MAINSTREAMING SCIENCE AND MATHEMATICS   *Special Ideas and Activities for*
the Whole Class
Charles R. Coble, Paul B. Hounshell, Anne H. Adams

THE OTHER SIDE OF THE REPORT CARD   *A How-to-Do-It Program for Affective Education*
Larry Chase

SELF-SCIENCE
Karen F. Stone and Harold Q. Dillehunt

THE WHOLE COSMOS CATALOG OF SCIENCE ACTIVITIES   *For Kids of All Ages*
Joe Abruscato and Jack Hassard

For information about these, or Goodyear books in Language Arts, Reading, General
Methods, and Centers, write to

Janet Jackson
Goodyear Publishing Company
1640 Fifth Street
Santa Monica, CA 90401
(213) 393-6731

Mathmatters

DEVELOPING COMPUTATIONAL
SKILLS WITH DEVELOPMENTAL
ACTIVITY SEQUENCES

Randall J. Souviney, Phd.

Teacher Education Program
University of California, San Diego

Tamara Keyser

Teacher and Curriculum Consultant
San Diego, California

Alan Sarver

Teacher, Willow Tree School
Idaho Falls, Idaho

Goodyear Publishing Company, Inc.
Santa Monica, California

**We dedicate this book to
all our students, from
whom we've learned so much.**

Library of Congress Cataloging in Publication Data
Souviney, Randall.
 Mathmatters.

 1. Mathematics—Study and teaching (Elementary)
I. Keyser, Tamara, joint author. II. Sarver,
Alan, joint author. III. Title.
QA135.5.S576   372.7'2   78-3535
ISBN 0-87620-601-1
ISBN 0-87620-600-3 pbk.
Y-6011-4 (case)
 6003-1 (paper)

Current Printing (last digit):
10 9 8 7 6 5 4 3 2 1

Book production by Ken Burke & Associates
Text and cover designer: Christy Butterfield
Illustrators: Jessica Bradley and Victoria Ann Philp
Compositor: Publications Services, Palo Alto, California

Contents

Preface

This book has been designed for those concerned with the development of mathematical skills in children. At issue is a rising dissatisfaction with the current pedagogical tendency to define elementary mathematics curricula as a sequence of well-defined behavorial objectives. Behavioral objectives, by their very nature, reflect only that knowledge which can be tested objectively. Knowledge most central to the study of elementary mathematics—namely, the proper approach to problem solving and analysis—is frequently neglected in favor of easily assessed skill-related concepts such as number facts and computation. Of course, no one seriously concerned with the education of children minimizes the importance of such skills. Nevertheless, if the teaching of mathematical concepts at the elementary level is confined to communicating only those ideas and skills that are easily tested, those concepts may come to be looked upon as maximum educational standards rather than minimum mathematical competencies.

In light of this trend, the need for a humanistic approach to teaching computational skills that is consistent with how children learn mathematics becomes especially apparent. The theory and technology necessary for the development of such a curriculum have existed for some time. What has been lacking is a management system that encourages extensive student-and-teacher interaction and places realistic demands on the teacher's time.

It is hoped that the reader will experience as much success as we have with these classroom activities. Your efforts will be rewarded by a newfound confidence in the eyes of the children in your care.

T.J.K.
A.G.S.
R.J.S.

Introduction

*Without interchange of thought and cooperation
with others, the individual would never come to
group his operations into a coherent whole.*

Jean Piaget[1]

Over the past decade, many innovations in curriculum and instructional techniques have been developed in order to help teachers better educate our youth. Some innovations, such as the open classroom, the integrated day, and developmentally consistent instruction, were imported from other countries. Well-known math programs, built on a foundation of "discovery," "inquiry," "unifying concepts," "higher math," or "programmed instruction," were developed at universities here in the United States. Publishers have influenced our interpretations of the new math with each succesive edition of the text-books. Politicians have nurtured our fondness for behavioral objectives and our concern for cost-effectiveness. The educational community itself has perpetrated the mania for individualized instruction, diagnostic/prescriptive laboratories, and a host of other innovations imposed upon the children in our schools.

Each of these pedagogical panaceas has proved beneficial in isolated situations; however, the great majority of classroom teachers are not fully committed to their implementation and use. Many have simply maintained a low professional posture, waiting for the new program to be slowly adapted to local needs and thereby rendered innocuous. Little successful long-range implementation of these "innovative" programs has permeated the educational community.

Much of the blame for the failure of the "new curriculum" and the "new pedagogy" lies with the lack of proper preservice and in-service teacher training. In fact, very little of the total educational budget in the United States is spent on in-service training. Most industries whose technology changes as rapidly as the technology of education spend a far greater proportion of their income on staff development. One constantly wonders how the spending of hundreds of millions of dollars in order to make computers calculate in nanoseconds can be justified when some children are barely able to calculate at all!

All major instigators of curriculum reform have attempted to accomplish one objective: to discover the instructional techniques used by successful teachers and to communicate those techniques so that they may be implemented by other teachers in the field. "Teacher-proof" packets were one popular means of accomplishing this task. The primary benefit derived from

---

[1]Jean Piaget, *The Origins of Intelligence in Children* (New York: International Press, 1952).

these packets was that the teacher did not need any training to use them. If students failed to learn, it was the packet that was reevaluated and improved upon, not the teacher. Learning packets were cost-effective, they were available for all subject areas—and the students liked them.

What has happened to learning packets? They are alive and well in diagnostic/prescriptive teaching (DPT) laboratories throughout the country. DPT labs can be recognized by the presence of a large wall covered with small cubbyholes. Each box holds a different work sheet, either pre- or post-test, that is carefully designed to "teach" or "test" a specific objective. The child's objective is to progress from the upper left-hand box to the lower right-hand box in six years. The teacher is there to check the work sheets, answer questions, provide pre- and postdiagnostic/prescriptive tests, and record the results. Since the curriculum is predetermined, the teacher's role is reduced—in many cases, to little more than that of a clerk.

These laboratories provide a very lonely environment for an eight-year-old with a learning problem. It is possible for weeks to go by without a teacher really talking to a student. The day may come when a child will be placed in one of these learning laboratories and in twelve years walk out with a high-school diploma. It is little wonder that children in our schools rebel when confronted with such inhuman approaches to education.

What seems to be missing in this and other examples of instructional innovation is the interaction between teachers and students. Though the premise that places priority on the meeting of individual needs may be indisputable, inappropriate application of this principle may be counterproductive. Many individualized programs make great demands on teachers' time, requiring shuffling of papers, pre- and post-testing, and recording of data. Little time remains for the vital interaction necessary for quality education. Any curriculum that attempts to meet individual needs must not do so at the expense of human interaction. Talking, discussing, comparing, questioning, arguing, inquiring, and loving must not take second place to meeting objectives, updating the checklist, completing the packet, and passing the post-test.

Consider the following situation as an example of inappropriate emphasis on individual needs:

> Imagine that you and some colleagues teaching in Los Angeles were each given twenty dollars to attend the Conference on New Teaching Fads and Gimmicks in San Francisco, each in your own individual manner. A few hours after you and your fellow teachers begin your journeys, one of you will be on the edge of Los Angeles, hitchhiking north; others will have formed a car pool and chosen to drive by way of Interstate 5; someone else will wind up penniless and stranded at the Fresno Airport; and another may find himself halfway to St. Louis.
>
> Since the objective is clearly to reach San Francisco, perhaps the best way to get everyone to the conference on time is to put them all on a bus and drive them there yourself!

Individualization means different things to different people, but even more important than varying the method to fit the student is varying the instructional technique according to the problem to be solved.

Not all problems are best solved by an individual working alone; nor can large groups be effective when utilizing a technique meant to vary with each student's unique personality. The imposition of techniques deemed superior by some outside expert will not uniformly provide results superior to each teacher's own well-established procedures.

The ideal objectives of individualized instruction are commendable and perhaps indisputable. It is the practical application of individualized techniques that should cause concern. The primary goal of the educational community might be phrased in the following manner: *To facilitate a sense of independence and competence in the lives of children.* But if the ultimate goal of individualization is indeed to create a unique curriculum for each child based upon some objective criterion (a goal which, in effect, may isolate children from each other and from their teacher), then the educational community may be defeating its most prized purpose. There is little justification for reducing, over extended periods of time, the quality or quantity of human interaction in order to individualize instruction.

Techniques are needed which provide for individual differences but do not unduly upset the established classroom routine. Caution in initiating a new program is especially important in the case of older children who have been socialized into ''appropriate'' school behavior for several years. If one attempts prematurely to provide diversified learning experiences through the use of learning centers, performance contracts, or other techniques of individualized instruction, the results may prove disappointing for everyone involved.

Though establishment of a unique curriculum for each child is theoretically possible, it is impractical at best and perhaps totally undesirable. Extensive classroom interaction must take place for education to become anything more than a committing to memory of meticulously structured, but functionally useless, facts. Without extensive human interaction, the development of concepts may be incomplete; and problem solving, commonly considered the most vital form of learning, may not take place.

Techniques for individualization presently used in the United States can be classified into three types (See Table I). Each type has several real and imagined advantages and disadvantages.

Type A is characterized by a curriculum in which every child works on a different concept at his own pace. Providing a curriculum consistent with this objective necessitates effective manipulation of the three dimensions associated with individualized instruction (see Fig. 1). Each child may work

1. on a different concept

2. at a different developmental level

3. during various times throughout the daily classroom schedule

The simultaneous varying of all three dimensions is currently purported to be the ultimate goal for the enlightened teacher. Few other educational goals give rise to as much unwarranted guilt in the total teaching population as have the recent attempts to apply this noble principle to all public-school classrooms. (There are other aspects of a teacher's responsibility that more properly justify feelings of guilt and elicit much more efficient use of time and emotion.)

TABLE I

Types of Individualized Instruction

DIMENSIONS VARIED

Type A	*Type B*	*Type C*
1. Concept	1. Concept	1. Developmental level
2. Time schedule	2. Time schedule	
3. Developmental level		

INSTRUCTIONAL ADVANTAGES

Type A	*Type B*	*Type C*
1. Every child works at own speed	1. Fewer activities to prepare than with Type A	1. Fewer activities to prepare than with Types A and B
2. Every child begins where he left off	2. Fewer groups and broader objectives facilitate student assessment	2. Student-and-teacher interaction encouraged
3. Effective for lower cognitive learning (i.e., multiplication tables and algorithms)	3. Fewer classroom-management problems	3. Less negative connotation associated with ability grouping
	4. Some student interaction encouraged	4. Many individual learning needs met
		5. Classroom management simplified
		6. Transition from traditional classroom procedures facilitated

INSTRUCTIONAL DISADVANTAGES

Type A	Type B	Type C
1. Requires extensive teacher time for preparing appropriate learning experiences	1. May not meet individual student needs since all students do all activities	1. Curriculum not completely tailored to individual needs
2. Student assessment is time consuming and often inaccurate	2. Initially, students have difficulty participating in activities not directly supervised by the teacher	2. Three activities must be designed for each concept instructed
3. Classroom-management problems recur	3. Activity instruction must be simple and complete, making process-type activities difficult to implement	
4. Ineffective for process or conceptual learning (i.e., problem solving, analysis, generalization, or classification)	4. Additional preparation required, while advantages gained over traditional large-group instruction are only minimal	
5. Teacher-and-student interaction reduced		
6. Behavioral-objective curriculum soon becomes the knowledge ceiling instead of the minimum standard		

EXAMPLES

Type A	Type B	Type C
1. Diagnostic/prescriptive teaching	1. Many "open space" curricula	1. Developmental activity sequences
2. Behavioral-objective inventories	2. Departmental instruction	
3. Programmed texts		
4. Computer-aided instruction		

Certain pedagogical advantages and disadvantages are apparent in Type A instruction. It is especially appropriate, for example, in short-term remedial situations and in cases when a student is confined due to illness or physical disability, or is isolated in an extreme rural area. The dehumanization inherent in such techniques suggests that they should not be used as ongoing means of instruction over long periods of time.

Examples of this type of individualized format abound in both commercially and locally developed forms. Terms commonly associated with such programs include *diagnostic/prescriptive teaching, behavioral-objective inventories, programmed texts,* and *computer-aided instruction.* These examples should not be confused with the British "integrated day" concept, which is designed to provide for individual needs but not at the expense of activity and interaction. At-

FIGURE 1   THREE DIMENSIONS OF INDIVIDUALIZED INSTRUCTION

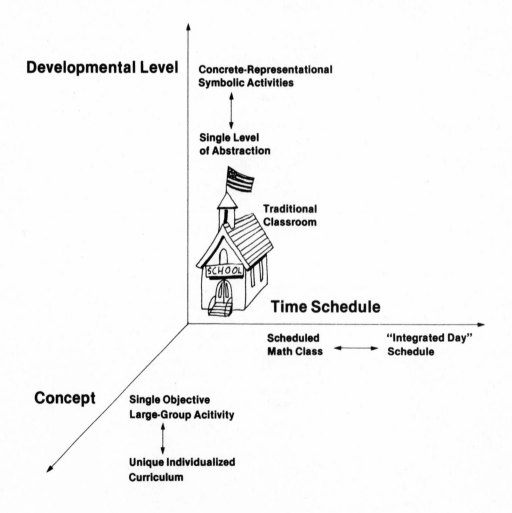

tempts at utilizing this model in public schools in the United States have not met with widespread success, chiefly because the emphasis placed on basic skills and memorization here seems to limit the method's effectiveness.

Type B individualized instruction is characterized by equal numbers of children working in groups and rotating through a sequence of activities. Generally the teacher is stationed with one group while the other groups work independently or with a classroom aide. Only the concept and time schedule dimensions vary in the Type B approach; each concept is generally presented at one developmental level.

Many "open space" classrooms, and departmentalized instruction at all levels, utilize some or all of these principles. Though little benefit over traditional large-group instruction is apparent with long-term application, Type B instruction may be appropriate where specialized teachers are scarce. Frequently this form of individualized instruction is mistakenly purported to meet individual needs, in spite of the fact that little attention is paid to the developmental abilities of each child.

In order to effectively utilize the third approach to individualized instruction (Type C), it must be recognized that few children are so unique that it is impossible for them to work with others for limited periods of time on specific concepts or topics. In the Type C method, groups of various sizes (sometimes one large group) are established based on some common need and maintained over a reasonable period of time (generally one to four weeks). Though the makeup of these groups does change with time and concept, groups generally remain together for a duration of time sufficient to encourage extensive peer interaction. Only one of the dimensions of individualization is varied at a time, allowing simplified classroom-management procedures.

This type of individualized format allows the teacher who may be dissatisfied with traditional instructional methods to institute a carefully controlled transition from a large-group, "teach-to-the-average" format to a manageable system of instruction that takes into account the individual differences of the students. Students and teachers have ample opportunity to adjust to any changes in classroom organization in an environment where interaction between the teacher and the students is encouraged.

One effective example of Type C instruction is the *developmental activity sequence* (see Fig. 2).[2] In utilizing developmental activity sequences, the time and concept dimensions are held constant while the developmental level is varied. All children work on the same concept at the same scheduled time but at different conceptual levels. Meeting individual needs in this manner is theoretically sound and functionally viable. Individualizing by accounting for various developmental levels meets the needs of particular children more fully than do approaches centered around concept- or time-schedule variations. The first section of this book provides specific suggestions for the implementation of such a program—specifically, one designed to teach computational skills. The

---

[2] Randall J. Souviney, "A New Commitment to Developmental Learning," *Learning Magazine,* March 1975.

second section provides detailed developmental activity sequences for the major concepts associated with computation skills from kindergarten through the sixth-grade level.

FIGURE 2   MODEL OF A DEVELOPMENTAL ACTIVITY SEQUENCE

Objective: A statement indicating that students will demonstrate understanding of a single clearly defined mathematical concept on at least one of the developmental levels below.

Activity 1:   Concrete Level

Concrete materials which, through manipulation, provide a clearly perceived model of the concept.

Activity 2:   Representational Level

Graphic or concrete materials which require greater use of the imagination in order to provide a model for the concept addressed.

Activity 3:   Symbolic Level

Letters, numerals, or other symbols which require abstract conceptualization without dependence on tangible models.

A MODEL
FOR LEARNING

Developmental Learning Theory [1]

Before creation and implementation of developmental activity sequences are described, it may be instructive to examine the Piagetian model of intellectual development. Developmental learning theory, based on the work of Jean Piaget, addresses itself to the manner in which a child characteristically views the world at each level of his intellectual development. Piaget divides this development into four levels (age divisions are only rough approximations):

1. Children from age zero to age two are considered to be functioning at the sensorimotor developmental level. Children at this level are developing reflex activity and hand-to-mouth coordination. External objects are imaged internally, and it is realized that they are one object among many objects in the world.

2. Children from age two to six are considered to be functioning at the preoperational level. Children at this level develop language skills. They establish relationships between an action and its results by trial-and-error methods. Though they are unable to solve conservation problems by reversing transformations, they do have the ability to classify objects logically. Nevertheless, they seldom allow for set inclusion or intersection (see Appendix II).

3. Children from age seven to eleven are functioning at the concrete operational level, the implications of which are therefore most important to elementary school teachers. Development at this level is characterized by the ability to interact with situations, learn by one's own mistakes, and organize learned information so that it may be used in solving new problems. At this stage, the child can solve conservation problems, classify concrete objects logically, and perceive set inclusion and intersection. He is still, however, unable to evaluate a situation systematically or to infer additional implications in order to describe other possible outcomes. For example, in explaining why two objects of different mass fall at the same rate, a child at the concrete operational level might not take air resistance into account and would be quite surprised when a large piece of plywood dropped horizontally proved to fall more slowly than a golf ball. Also, children at this level are likely to confuse variables or change more than one variable at a time when evaluating cause-effect relationships. For example, if asked to adjust the frequency of a pendulum, a child will generally adjust the weight of the pendulum, whereas the length is the variable that affects the frequency. In adjusting the weight, however, he may simultaneously adjust the length and attribute the change in frequency to the change in the weight.

---

1. "A New Commitment to Developmental Learning." Portions of this section have been reprinted by special permission of *Learning, The Magazine for Creative Teaching*, March, 1975. Copyright © 1975 by Education Today Company, Inc., 530 University Avenue, Palo Alto, CA 94301.

4. Between twelve and fourteen years of age, children pass into the final stage of development, the formal (symbolic) operational level. This level is characterized by the ability to solve complex verbal and written problems. At this stage, children can classify objects according to abstract attributes; differentiate between variables, testing them one at a time to determine causality; and generalize results to cover all possible situations.

Developmental theory suggests that instructional methods and materials must be appropriate to a child's level of development. Therefore, for each major concept taught, teachers should have at their disposal a series of activities that spans the developmental range of the students. Curriculum design at the elementary-school level must be consistent with the ability of children at the concrete operational level. Activities designed to extend conceptual understanding to the formal operational level are of equal importance. It should be pointed out that since the developmental level is not fixed according to age, experiential activities consistent with the preoperational level may be called for at all grade levels.

It is often the case that, while concrete activities involving manipulative materials are used to introduce a concept, instruction involving extension of the concept is carried out at the symbolic level. For example, first graders may be introduced to addition through use of a balance, union of concrete sets, or at least a representational number line. Very soon, however, children are doing page after page of examples in order to reinforce the original concept. There is substantial research to support the contention that considerably more experiences with concrete activities are necessary in order to lay a strong foundation for symbolic manipulation.

Model for Learning

Through contrast of the stages of intellectual development as described by Piaget and Bruner,[2] a model for conceptualizing the learning process and guidelines for appropriate learning experiences become apparent (Table II). The developmental stages as described by Piaget—concrete, representational, and symbolic—make up the horizontal axis. The vertical axis is comprised of three types of learning experiences as described by Bruner— remembered experiences, problem solving, and independent investigation. Each cell represents one of the nine types of learning situations available to classroom teachers.

Developmental theory suggests that children operating at the concrete level ought to be given considerable experience utilizing concrete conceptual models prior to involving them with representational and symbolic activities. Similarly, Bruner suggests that children need to experience situations without being given designated objectives (free exploration) before they are assigned specific problems or are required to create their own problem situations.

2. Robert Wirtz, *Mathematics for Everyone* (Washington, D.C.: Curriculum Development Associates, 1974).

It is interesting to note that most current mathematics curricula utilize learning activities characterized in Table II as symbolic/problem solving (Type 6), though occasionally we may find some concept development at the representational level of problem solving (Type 5). The goal of this book is to reverse current instructional trends. According to the method outlined herein, a concept is introduced by means of perceptually based concrete models; symbolic manipulations are developed subsequently. The goal of this book is to put this model, presently utilized in remedial cases only, into universal practice.

It is suggested that instruction begin with Type 1, free-exploration activities whose purpose is to familiarize students with the concrete materials. After this first step toward problem solving has been accomplished, the teacher provides a developmental activities sequence (DAS) for each concept being considered. These are represented by Types 4, 5, and 6 in Table III. In order to provide for varying rates of individual-student progress, the teacher must encourage children who quickly become competent at a particular activity to generate their own problems, i.e., to embark upon independent investigation (Types 7, 8, and 9). This step deepens conceptual understanding before representational or symbolic activities are undertaken. The ultimate goal is to have the children doing independent investigation at the symbolic level. The importance of symbolic/independent investigation as a goal, a direction, must be remembered. It is an activity that many *adults* are unable to handle effectively. Though symbolic/problem solving may be an appropriate objective for the vast majority of our students, independent investigation must continue to be the primary goal of our instructional programs. Priorities must be set to ensure that problem solving will always be looked upon as a minimum student competency.

Meeting Individual Needs

Each child in your classroom has a unique developmental makeup based upon his or her own personal history. In addition, the developmental level at which a child operates will vary according to concept. Consider the mathematical concept of addition with regrouping, itself dependent upon the concept of place value. Curricula that call for the introduction of place value at age six and the formalization of the concept at age seven assume that the child is able to discriminate relative numeral values according to position. He must be able to determine, for example, in the numeral 23, which is larger, the 2, or the 3. It is not developmentally sound to assume that a child of seven will consistently choose the 2 when considering the symbol 23. However, when the problem is displayed in a concrete manner (i.e., with a manipulative model) the child at the concrete level is better able to conceptualize the problem and provide a successful solution. This child may be able to solve sums that don't call for regrouping using only symbols,

$$
\begin{array}{r}
14 \\
+11 \\
\hline
25
\end{array}
$$

TABLE II

DEVELOPMENTAL MODEL FOR LEARNING

DEVELOPMENTAL LEVEL				
		Concrete	*Representational*	*Symbolic*
PROBLEM MODE	*Remembered Experiences*	1. **Free Exploration** **Play** **Discovery**	2. **Recognizing Pictures**	3. **Early Language Development**
	Problem Solving	4. **Concrete Experiences**	5. **Lessons Utilizing** **Pictures and Graphics**	6. **Most Textbooks** **Worksheets**
	Independent Investigation	7. **Laboratory Experiences**	8. **Creative Art**	9. **Creative Writing** **Inferential Research**

TABLE III

DEVELOPMENTAL ACTIVITY SEQUENCES

DEVELOPMENTAL LEVEL				
		Concrete	*Representational*	*Symbolic*
	Remembered Experiences	1. **Begin Instruction**	2.	3.
	Problem Solving	4.	5.	6.
			Developmental Activity Sequence	
	Independent Investigation	**Independent Investigation**	**Independent Investigation**	**Independent Investigation**

PROBLEM MODE

But he may require help from tile strips or Cuisenaire rods in order to consistently find answers to sums that call for regrouping.

$$\begin{array}{r} 39 \\ + 27 \\ \hline 66 \end{array}$$

An additional comment should be made in regard to developmental level. The notion of a child's "being at the concrete operational level" or "being at the preoperational level" is less than accurate. *Developmental level* is spoken of in relation to a particular task or concept rather than to the child as a whole. An individual may be at the concrete operational level in reference to area measurement but at the formal operational level when dealing with the concept of classification. This implies that teachers must be careful not to prejudge the developmental level of a child with reference to any particular concept. Certainly, familiarity with a child's past accomplishments provides the teacher with considerable insight. Nevertheless, each child must have ample opportunity to experience a concept at various developmental levels.

Application with Older Children

The application of developmentally consistent instruction is as important in the education of children ages eight to twelve as it is for younger children. Indeed, secondary and university curricula would profit if teachers made appropriate use of concrete and representational experiences prior to introducing concept formation. Oftentimes, teachers feel that students in the upper elementary grades should be capable of solving symbolic problems after only a brief introductory experience with concrete models. This should indeed be the case with many children. What is not taken into account, however, is that the normal development of a good number of children has been hampered by lack of experience with concrete models and/or by premature introduction to symbolic representation. If concept development involving manipulative experiences with concrete materials is not provided at the primary level, it must be provided by the teacher at the time that the lack of experience is discovered.

Several years ago, while I was teaching in Santee, California, a boy who had recently moved to California from the Midwest was placed in my eighth-grade math class. Since he was consistently unable to solve simple arithmetic problems presented on prepared work sheets, my colleagues and I were concerned with his cognitive aptitude. His behavior on the playground, however, showed him to be so well coordinated that he would often take leadership roles in games. He worked well with tools in shop and in the five weeks he was with us, learned to play a good game of chess. Test scores confirmed (?) that his intelligence and ability were "normal." Our astonishment was acute, then, when, upon giving him some of Piaget's conservation tasks to determine his approximate developmental level, we discovered he was unable to conserve length, mass, area, displacement, or volume or to deal effectively with class inclusion. Needless to say, I spent an exciting and oftentimes frustrating year trying to invent concrete activities that were not socially demeaning yet dealt with the elementary concepts he had left behind.

By the end of that year, the boy was able to conserve length and area and deal effectively with set inclusion. His growth can be attributed to a multitude of measurement activities adapted to his need over this period of time. He was always in charge of chalking the lines of the ball fields, for example; and one class project in which he was involved called for measuring and making a map of the school campus. These and many other concrete activities provided him with some of the experience he lacked, resulting in considerable growth in his problem-solving skills, his reasoning ability, and his self-confidence. He did indeed make a great deal of progress that year; nevertheless, it is feared that his view of the world will remain somewhat distorted due to deficiencies in his early experiences.

Though this example is admittedly extreme, most children lack some conceptual development that, if not properly dealt with, can cause serious learning difficulties later on. Certainly, determining a student's developmental level relative to a specific concept and providing appropriate instruction can help him to make important strides not only at the early stages of education, but at all stages.

The Developmental Activity Sequence

Developmental activity sequences (DAS) can be an effective and practical approach to meeting individual needs. The sequences described herein were designed to provide mathematics instruction consistent with the developmental abilities of children.

The DAS consists of a series of activities spanning the developmental range of the students. Formulated to instruct a single concept at various conceptual levels, the sequence may include an exploratory activity at the preoperational level; a concrete, manipulative activity at the concrete operational level; a representational activity utilizing pictures, sketches, or other representations of real objects as a transition between the concrete and formal levels; and finally, symbolic exercises utilizing written language and numerals at the formal operational level (see Fig. 2, p. xvi). Three or four properly chosen activities of the types described above will in most cases provide for the individual needs of the child while simplifying classroom-management procedures. All the children are working on the same concept at the same time yet at different developmental levels.

Summary

In order to more fully meet the needs of each child in his classroom without discouraging student interaction, the teacher must possess a basic understanding of how a child develops intellectually. Armed with the knowledge of developmental learning theory, he can then prepare a series of activities for each concept to be taught, spanning the anticipated developmental range of the students. From kindergarten through sixth grade, exploratory activities for each concept should begin with concrete manipulation at the concrete operational level. Each succeeding level requires greater use of the child's imagination in order to facilitate conceptualization. A series of such activities designed to meet a single objective is called a *developmental activity sequence.*

Each child is allowed ample time and opportunity to work at each level. Once proficiency has been demonstrated, students are encouraged to develop their own problem situations and solutions and then to move on to the next level. The teacher must be aware that children will not necessarily progress at the same rate or develop the same degree of understanding. It should, however, be of some comfort to the teacher that conceptualization of a particular objective will always take place at some level, though perhaps not at the formal (symbolic) level, the ultimate goal of cognitive development.

How to Use This Book

The teacher who will make most effective use of the activities presented in the following chapters is the teacher who first tries them out himself. Familiarity with the entire set of experiences will allow him to optimize his presentations. If time doesn't allow for such luxuries, however, the best approach is to choose the sections that will be addressed during the year and go through each pertinent activity, constructing materials as required. A brief review of the topic immediately preceeding the topic of interest may also prove useful.

Keep the set of materials you develop in "rehearsal" to use as examples for your students. As a rule, it is extremely useful for the children to keep the materials in a safe place even after they have finished with them. Many materials are used over again in a different context and saving them will minimize reconstruction time.

Each child's development should be evaluated by means of the diagnostic activities described in Appendix I. Each of these necessitates working individually with each child for a few minutes in order to assess his intellectual competence with regard to various cognitive readiness skills. The teacher must also take care to consider the teaching implications presented by each task. The more thoroughly an educator is able to implement these suggestions, the greater the success he will experience with his students.

Once you are familiar with the activities, materials, and diagnostic procedures, you are ready to begin. At first all students should participate in every activity in the sequence, spending as much time as necessary on each. Later, as the teacher becomes more familiar with his students' individual abilities and developmental competencies, he can direct each child to the appropriate activity from the outset. Once children begin a developmental series (at whatever level is appropriate), they should be allowed to work through each subsequent activity from that point on. Also, as children become competent at a particular activity, they should be encouraged to develop their own problem situations before attempting the next activity.

Once you become familiar with the techniques presented, additional activities may be attempted. In order to create one's own developmental activity sequences, it is necessary to develop skill in utilizing some of the vast array of concrete materials available for use in the classroom (see Appendix III). Many of the best materials are student or teacher made and therefore inexpensive.

Section II of this volume is comprised of detailed instructions for approximately fifty activity sequences designed to provide children with the opportunity to experience computational concepts at several levels of abstraction. You need not restrict your program to the activities and materials suggested herein—as there are several approaches to meeting each objective. Consider these activities as starting points, adapting them as necessary to your style and to the materials you have available.

Never forget that every child will not achieve symbolic conceptualization unless ample time is allowed at each activity level. This time requirement may vary greatly from child to child; indeed, developmental theory suggests that acquisition of symbolic understanding may not take place until much later in the child's life. Work above all toward developing activities that are varied and stimulating, especially when the children involved remain at one level for long periods of time.

DEVELOPMENTAL ACTIVITY SEQUENCES

Developing Whole-Number Concepts

As children mature intellectually, they assign meaning to their environment with increasing internal consistency. Development of this rational perspective is an essential foundation for the teaching of mathematics, and the ability to quantify appropriate facets of one's world is a primary building block. Young children must develop understanding of the abstract notions of number before they can possibly begin to exercise this perspective. Research suggests that children first order their world according to physical attributes that are more immediately measurable than is number. These would include any properties that the child could compare by touch, smell, sight, sound, or even taste. Activities in Topic 1 provide for guided experience with this type of classification (see Appendix I for a more complete discussion of whole-number readiness skills). Children are asked to order familiar objects according to specified attributes, i.e., color, size, texture, or shape.

Through such experiences, children develop the ability to generalize information, and multiple comparisons soon become possible. Skill in comparing and ordering several objects according to one attribute, referred to as a *seriation,* is prerequisite to a meaningful understanding of numerousness. In Topic 1, children are asked to seriate strips of M & M's according to length. Other possible exercises include ordering the class by height—or perhaps by foot size.

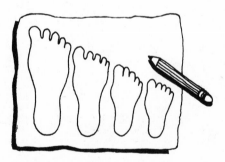

Children should be encouraged to look for such means of classification in other curriculum areas as well. Any attribute lends itself to this type of activity. For example, if the story of *Charlotte's Web* is read aloud, the class could be asked what animals resemble the heroine spider and how they are similar. Do they have spiny legs? Do they crawl? Perhaps they can be classified together because they are brave or brilliant.

Extensive classificational experiences of this type motivate children's efforts to order objects according to more abstract, quantifiable attributes. Instrumental in the development of this ability is the child's understanding of a number's invariance, generally referred to as *conservation.* This skill allows children to work with sets instead of simply classifying singular objects. They are taught that sets become similar when they contain the same number of objects, regardless of the objects' individual physical characteristics. In this manner, the concept of whole number becomes a natural extension of a child's perception of his or her physical environment.

Concept A: Exploration of Groups and Grouping

Activity 1-A1.
(concrete)

•*Materials* Glue, construction paper (divided in half), a collection of objects.

•***Procedure*** Have students go outside and collect a group of similar objects—leaves, rocks, sticks, etc.—which they are then to bring back to the classroom. Each child has his own piece of construction paper, which is divided into two parts. Students are asked to divide their objects into two groups in *any* way they choose.

Student's Collection

Student's Classification

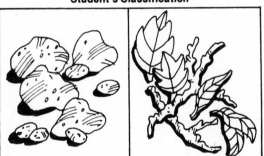

While the students are grouping their objects, ask them questions about their classifications: "Why did you put these objects all together?" "Why is this object in this group?" Such questioning encourages verbalization of the specific attributes that students are recognizing.

If time is available, write the students' comments on their respective papers. This encourages symbolic-language development and enhances a child's reading skills.

Activity 1-A2.
(concrete/
representational)

•*Materials*   Old magazines, paper, paste, scissors.

•*Procedure*   Students go through old magazines, cutting out any pictures they like. Again they are asked to divide these pictures in two groups, *any* way they choose.

The students will start to use words and phrases like "same," "not the same," "alike," "different," "go together," etc. The development of this vocabulary should be reinforced and encouraged. Students then paste their pictures onto construction paper that has been divided in two parts.

Once again, the teacher should record each student's comments.

These are like each other because you can eat them.

These are the same because they are things that grow outside that you can't eat.

•*Materials*   Groups of objects, paper, pencils.

Note: The symbolic stage is reached after extensive experience in the concrete and representational phases. It is first introduced as a recording procedure—a more efficient method of handling information. Accordingly, this activity is divided into two parts. The first part (A) is for use with younger students (that is, when these activities are used as the primary introduction to these concepts). Generally students at this level will not have begun reading or writing; therefore, any recording procedure must be done by means of pictures. The second part (B) is for those students who have had some reading experience as well as for those using these sequences for corrective work.

•*Procedure A*   Have the students divide objects into two groups. The activity is more effective if these objects are large and cumbersome—tables, chairs, and so forth. The students are asked how they could show their parents the groups they have made. Eventually they will arrive at the idea of taking pictures or making drawings of the groups. The concept being developed is that concrete groupings may be recorded symbolically to provide a means for more efficient communication. Have the students record their results on paper divided into two parts.

•*Procedure B*   Follow the same procedure as outlined above, asking similar questions but including a language-arts activity. Have the students label their groups with the actual symbols (i.e., words).

round table   rocking chair
square table   big chair
rectangular table   little chairs

Concept B: Grouping by Specific Attribute

Activity 1-B1.
(concrete)

•*Materials*   Three different shapes of macaroni, construction paper, markers, glue.

Possible Types of Macaroni

Shells   **Wheels**   **Curlicues**

•*Procedure*   Each bag of different-shaped noodles should be divided into thirds. Each third should be colored with food coloring, red, blue, or yellow. Mix the different shapes and colors together in one container. Place a randomly selected piece of macaroni on a piece of construction paper.

Blue Wheel

Ask a child to describe the piece you've chosen (Student: "That's a blue wheel"). Next ask him to pick out all the pieces in some way similar to the blue wheel and place them next to the blue wheel. They should have picked yellow and red wheels as well as blue curlicues and shells.

Yellow Wheel   **Blue Wheel**   **Red Wheel**

Blue Curlicue   **Blue Shell**

As students are selecting the macaroni, they should be asked to explain how each piece is like the blue wheel. The students will soon notice that there are two ways in which pieces can be "like" the blue wheel: by shape and by color.

After the attributes are named, draw two overlapping circles on the construction paper, labeling one *shape* and one *color*.

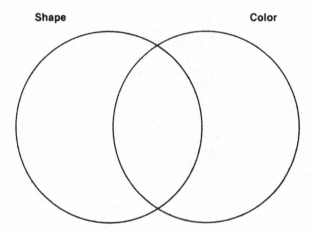

Shape   **Color**

Next have students select any piece of macaroni and glue it into the area where the circles overlap. Ask them to describe the piece they've chosen (Student: "I chose a red curlicue").

Now, you can label the circles with the two attributes the student has named.

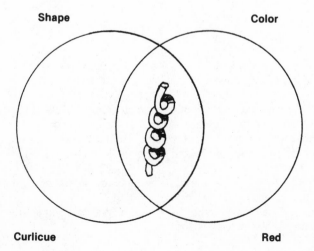

Shape   **Color**

Curlicue   **Red**

Ask the student to pick out all the types of macaroni that are "like" the red curlicue in some way, verbally describing each piece as they pick it out. Ask students to glue the pieces they have selected into the appropriate circles. The final product should look something like this:

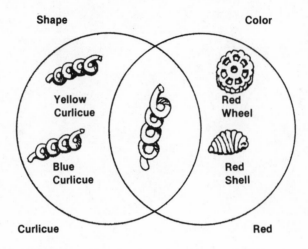

Students should be guided toward discovery and verbalization of the fact that a red curlicue must be placed in the overlapped area because it has both attributes, redness and "curlicueness."

Activity 1-B2.
(representational)

•*Materials*   Pictures from Work Sheet 1-B2 (eagle, bat, duck, walrus, fish, ostrich, horse, lizard), construction paper, pencils, glue, scissors.

•***Procedure***   Ask students to cut out all the animal pictures. Talk about each animal, its form of locomotion (flys, walks, or swims) and its type of "skin" (fur, scales, or feathers). It is important for this activity that children become familiar with each animal's body covering and mode of locomotion. (Ducks should be classified as swimmers.)

Put all the pictures in front of the student. Select one animal and place it on a piece of construction paper.

Ask students to pick out all the animals that are "like" the horse in some way. Have them place their pictures on the paper.

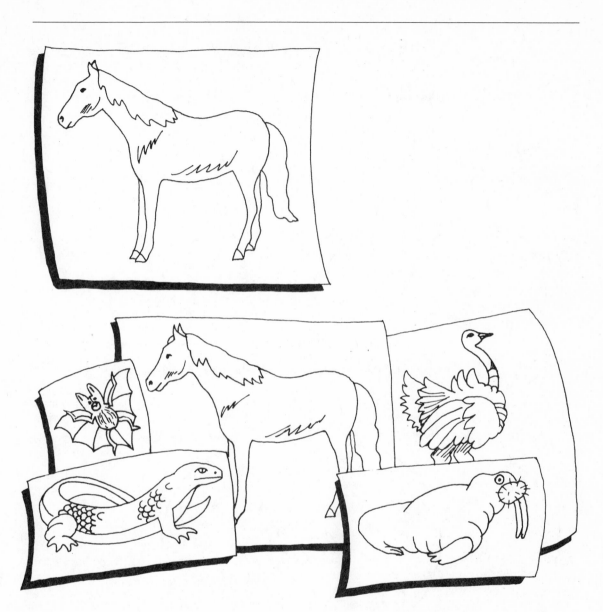

Students should explain the way in which each picture is like the horse: "The lizard is like the horse because he walks." "The bat is like the horse because it's got fur." "The ostrich is like the horse because it walks, too." "The walrus is like the horse because he has fur, too."

Students should discover and verbalize the fact that there are two ways in which the animals can be "like" the horse: they can have fur (same body covering) or they can walk (move the same way).

Now draw two overlapping circles and label them as below.

Movement   **Body Covering**

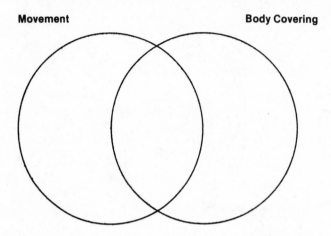

Have your students glue one of the pictures into the area where the circles overlap. They should label the circles according to the picture they have selected. If they have chosen the walrus, the circles would be labeled "swims" and "fur."

Movement   **Body Covering**

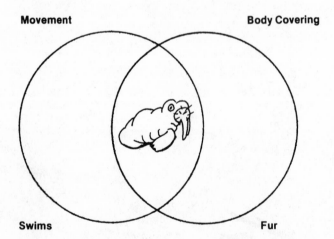

Swims   **Fur**

Next ask the students to pick out all the animals that are "like" the walrus in some way. Students should then decide which circle each of these pictures belongs in ("fur" or "swim"). They can then glue their pictures into the appropriate spots.

Movement   Body Covering

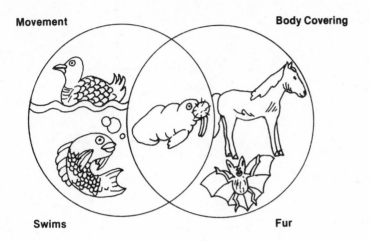

Swims   Fur

•*Materials*   Pencils, Work Sheet 1-B3.

•***Procedure***   Students are given Work Sheet 1-B3 and asked to classify each group of objects according to the specified criteria as they did in activities 1-B1 and 2.

Activity 1-B3.
(symbolic)

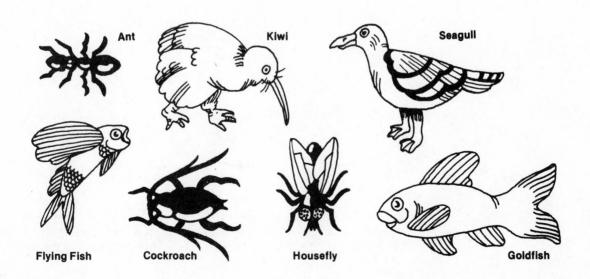

Ant   Kiwi   Seagull

Flying Fish   Cockroach   Housefly   Goldfish

Name_____

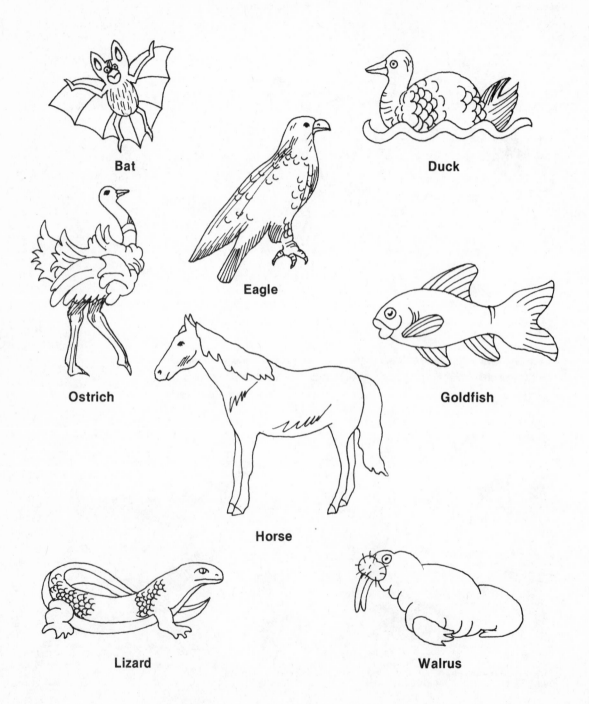

Bat

Duck

Eagle

Ostrich

Goldfish

Horse

Lizard

Walrus

Name_____

1.

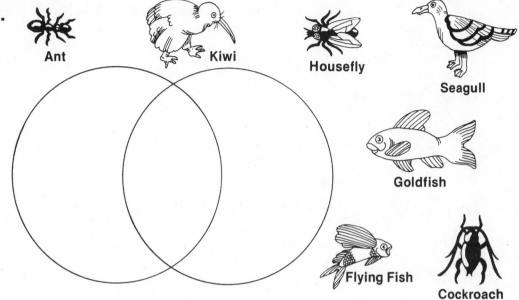

Ant   Kiwi   Housefly   Seagull

Goldfish

Flying Fish   Cockroach

2.

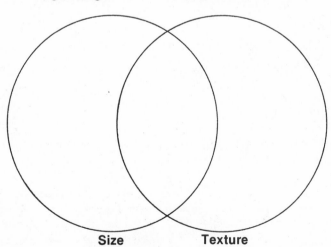

Large Rough Rock   Medium Smooth Rock

Small Rough Rock

Small Smooth Rock

Medium Rough Rock

Large Smooth Rock

Size   Texture

These animals can be classified as flying or nonflying birds, fish, or insects. Other classifications are also possible.

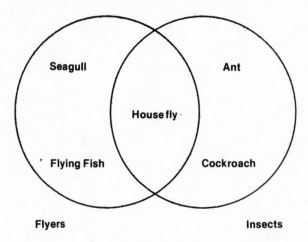

Students should be encouraged to write the names of the objects in the appropriate circles. If that is not feasible, however, they may draw pictures.

Concept C: One-to-One Correspondence

Activity 1-C1.
(concrete)

•*Materials*   Unifix cubes.

•**Procedure**   During a period of free exploration with Unifix cubes, students will naturally build towers. To explore one-to-one correspondence, have students copy teacher-built towers. Methods of comparison will be developed; comparison by length will naturally be most common. Since one-to-one correspondence is the concept being stressed, have students take the towers apart and place the cubes from each tower in two parallel rows, comparing the number of cubes one by one. Do not encourage counting at this time.

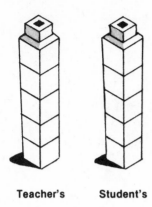

Teacher's   Student's

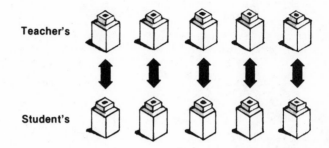

Teacher's

Student's

•*Materials*   Unifix cubes, objects to count, Record Sheet 1-C2.

•***Procedure***   Students are given Unifix cubes and asked to pick out one cube for each person in the group (including themselves) and build a tower. Once this has been accomplished, talk about the tower as representing the group of students. If students find this concept hard to grasp, have one of them take the tower apart, placing one cube in front of each member of the group.

Activity 1-C2.
(concrete/ representational)

This can also be done with cubes corresponding to the students' feet or hands; or cubes can represent every person wearing blue.

A very graphic example is the comparison of cubes and fingers.

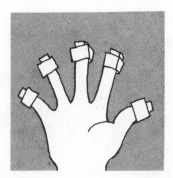

Have students record each situation on their recording sheet, coloring in the number of squares that corresponds to the number in their Unifix towers.

Name_____

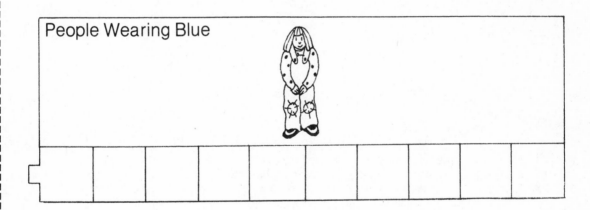

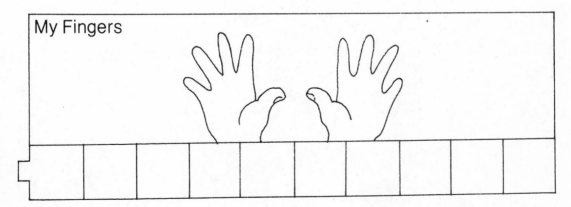

Activity 1-C3.
(representational)

•*Materials*   Unifix cubes, Record Sheet 1-C3.

•*Procedure*   Groups of students leave the classroom armed with bags of Unifix cubes. Each student builds a tower that corresponds one-to-one with a set of objects that he cannot bring back into the classroom. He then records his tower on a recording sheet and brings that back to be shared with the others. Towers could be built to represent the number of birds in the trees, the number of pill bugs in the bushes, the number of flowers in bloom, or the number of pleasant faces versus unpleasant faces they see (leave it to each student to decide what is or isn't a pleasant face). The significance of this activity is that the objects being counted never come into the classroom. The recording by means of the tower, whose cubes *represent* the objects, provides a significant step toward developing an abstract notion of number.

Activity 1-C4.
(representational/ symbolic)

•*Materials*   Baggies filled with various types of food—celery, carrots, raisins, peanuts, sunflower seeds (different numbers, one to nine, of each object)—Graph Sheet made up as shown in the figure on page 30, pencils (other sortable items may be substituted for food if desired).

Name_____

How many birds did you see?

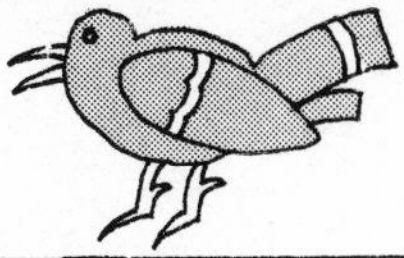

How many pill bugs were there?

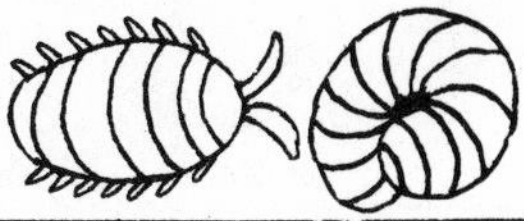

What kind of faces did you see people make?

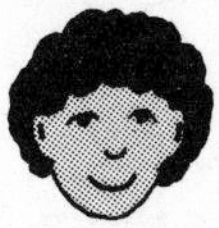

Pleasant

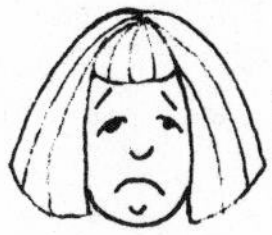

Unpleasant

•*Procedure*   Give students a bag of food each. Ask them to make a record of what they find, coloring one square for each item.

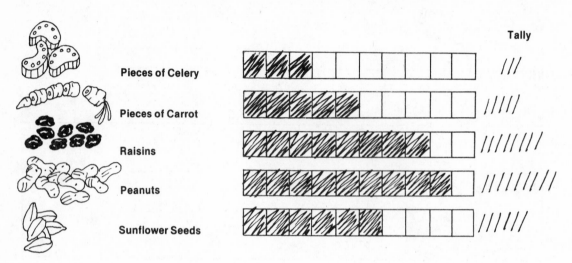

		Tally
Pieces of Celery		///
Pieces of Carrot		/////
Raisins		////////
Peanuts		/////////
Sunflower Seeds		//////

Once a student has made a record of his "food finds," ask him to tally up his results to the right of the appropriate squares. Once they have made a record, students can destroy the evidence!

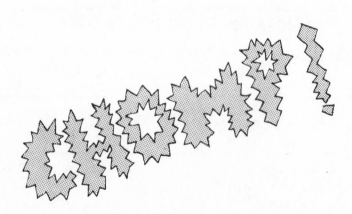

Concept D: Grouping by Number

• *Materials*   A set of tile strips (one through nine), extra tiles, cardboard strips, and glue.

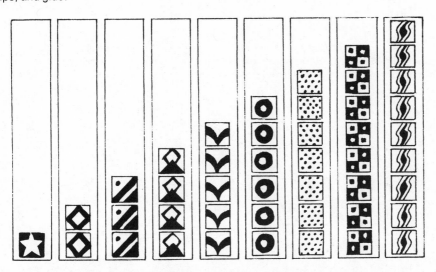

Note: If possible, have students make their own set of tile strips.

• *Procedure*   After a period of free exploration with tiles and tile strips, begin a matching game with the students by selecting a tile strip and having students match it by gluing additional tiles on cardboard.

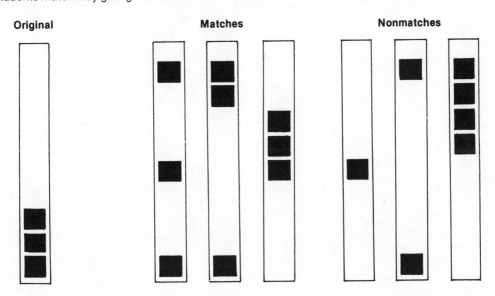

Original   Matches   Nonmatches

Do this with each of the nine tile strips. Notice that instead of size, shape, or color, the attribute which decides match or nonmatch is number alone. Matches are determined strictly by one-to-one comparison. Counting should not be encouraged.

Activity 1-D2.
(representational)

●*Materials*   Paper, paste, scissors, Work Sheet 1-D2.

●*Procedure*   Students examine work sheet and circle the groups of objects (each group contains one to nine objects).

Next, students cut out the various groups and paste those with like numbers onto separate cards.

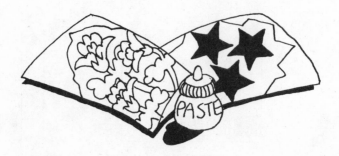

Again, counting is not encouraged. Grouping is done by comparison only. Students should be asked to explain why they are grouping their pictures in a particular way. These verbalizations can then be recorded by the teacher.

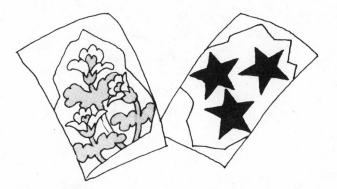

These are together because they all have the same number.

Concept E: Comparing Numbers

•*Materials*   Chairs, some open space.

•***Procedure***   Have a group of students sit on the floor. Line up chairs in front of them so that there is one more chair than there are students. Ask students whether there are enough, too few, or too many chairs for them all. Ask, "How could we find out?"

Activity 1-E1.
(concrete)

Name_____

One by one have students sit down on the chairs. Again ask whether there are too many, too few, or just enough for everybody. Repeat the activity, having students close their eyes while chairs are removed or added. Each time the students move to the chairs, ask, ''Are there more chairs or more people? How do you know? How can we make them equal?''

•*Materials*   Unifix cubes, objects to count.

•**Procedure**   Have students build towers of Unifix cubes with each cube representing concrete objects (see Activity 1-C3). Ask them to compare their towers using one-to-one correspondence to discover whether one has more, fewer than, or the same number of cubes as the others. For example, eight students' wearing blue and six students' wearing yellow would lead to construction of the following towers:

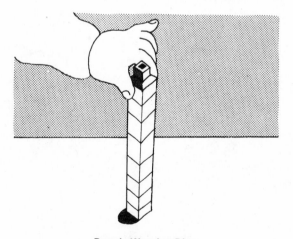
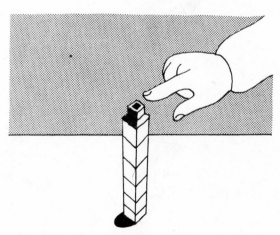

People Wearing Blue   **People Wearing Yellow**

Encourage students to verbalize their results. For example: ''There are more people wearing blue than wearing yellow'' or ''There are fewer people wearing yellow than blue.'' Also set up ''equal'' situations.

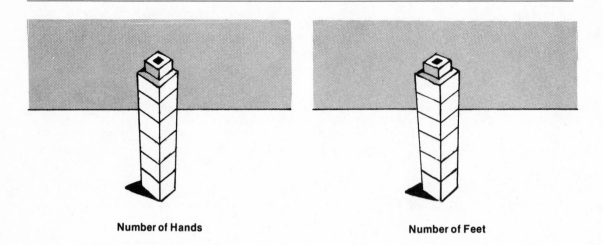

Number of Hands　　　　　　　　　　　　　　　**Number of Feet**

This could be verbalized as "There is the same number of hands as there is feet in this group."

Activity 1-E3.
(representational)

•*Materials*　A set of pictures with groups of objects ("crocodile food") in them, three crocodile heads (see graphics).

•*Procedure*　Students compare two pictures of objects, determining whether one has more than, fewer than, or the same number as the other.

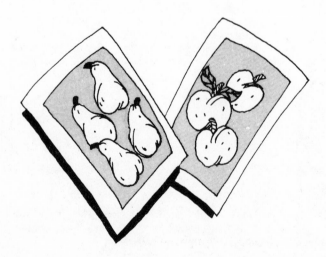

Next introduce Crockmorethan, Crocklessthan, and Crocksameas.

Since all crocodiles are greedy, they always eat the picture with the most objects in it. Pick two pictures from the deck of cards and place them on the table. Have a child put the appropriate crocodile between the object cards.

If the two object cards contain the same number of items, crocodiles get confused and close their mouths, eating neither card.

Ask students to tell you about these pictorial "number sentences" and record their responses.

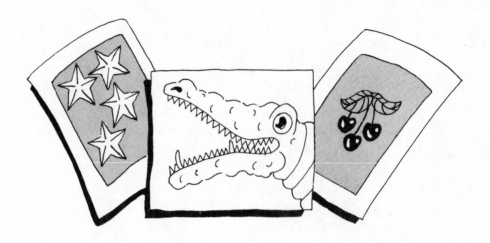

Activity 1-E4.
(symbolic)

•*Materials*   Paper, pencils, cards from Activity 1-E3, Work Sheet 1-E4.

Note: Only after extensive successful experience with the preceeding activities should children be encouraged to move on to the first symbolic activity.

•*Procedure*   Set up a picture-card situation for the students to solve.

After they have placed the proper croc-card, suggest that a record of the problems and answers should be kept. Ask how one might record this problem without using the picture cards. One possible recording procedure is to have the children make a tally of the number of objects and use the ''crocodile's mouth'' to indicate the comparison.

If children are familiar with the number names and symbols, record as follows:

Next, ask students to complete the work sheet, placing the proper crocodile symbol between each pair of objects and recording the situation either by tally or with numbers.

Name_____

Example

Record:
$$|| < |||$$

1.

Record:

2.

Record:

3.

Record:

4.

Record:

Concept F: Naming the Numbers

This concept deals with the transition between the representational and symbolic levels of number recognition. As such, it serves more as a capstone to the preceding activities than as a separate concept. While few of the foregoing activity sequences truly reached the symbolic level, the activities grouped under Concept F are either representational or symbolic. A familiarity with number names and extensive experience with the preceding activity sequences are necessary in order to continue.

•*Materials*   Unifix cubes.

Activity 1-F1.
(representational)

•***Procedure***   Students repeat Activity 1-C3, in which they are sent outside to build Unifix towers that represent a group of real objects or a set of occurrences. Upon their return, one tower is selected for examination.

Perhaps the tower represents the number of birds the students saw. The teacher says, "You saw three birds," and asks students to find other examples of threes. New towers are constructed so that a direct one-to-one comparison can always be made if necessary. This exercise should be repeated for numbers one through nine.

•*Materials*   Unifix cubes, picture cards from previous activities, index cards.

Activity 1-F2.
(representational)

•***Procedure***   Ask students to build Unifix towers that record the number of objects depicted on the picture cards and then to tally the numbers on 3″ × 5″ cards.

Children familiar with the number symbols may wish to use them instead of the tally marks. Other students should be introduced to the symbols at this time, e.g.,

The following activities will also help children develop numeral awareness.

a. Number Prints

•*Materials*   Tempera paint, paper towels, Work Sheet 1-F2a.

•*Procedure*   Students are given Work Sheet 1-F2a and a small (dixie cup) container of tempera. They are asked to put the appropriate number of tempera thumbprints under each numeral.

This exercise is even more fun when the teacher makes large butcher-paper charts on which students can make tempera footprints. (It's good to do this one outside.)

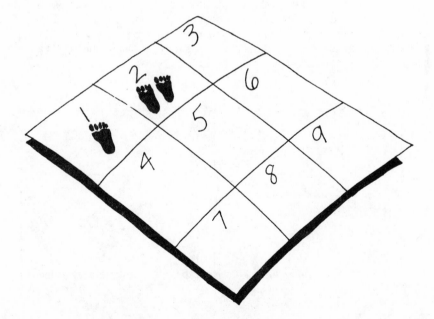

b. Popcorn Numbers

•*Materials*   Construction paper, popcorn, glue.

•*Procedure*   Teacher draws numerals on sheets of construction paper.

Students glue the appropriate numbers of popcorn kernels (or whatever material the teacher may choose: sand, pebbles, marshmallows) on their numbers.

c. Number Books

•*Materials*   Cornmeal or glitter in different colors, three-by-two-inch squares of construction paper with numerals 1–9 (an entire set for each student, with one number on each card), glue, stapler.

•***Procedure***   Teacher prepares number cards and cornmeal. (Mixing with a few drops of food coloring will color the cornmeal.) Students select construction-paper cards and put glue around the numerals. Next they sprinkle cornmeal onto the glue and let it dry. They repeat this for all the numerals and then staple them into a book.

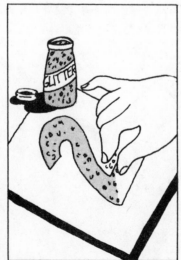

Name

1	2	3
4	5	6
7	8	9

Activity 1-F3.
(symbolic)

•*Materials*   Food graphs from 1-C4 (or similar graph), pencils, Work Sheet 1-F3.

•*Procedure*   Students examine their charts and add a new column for numerals.

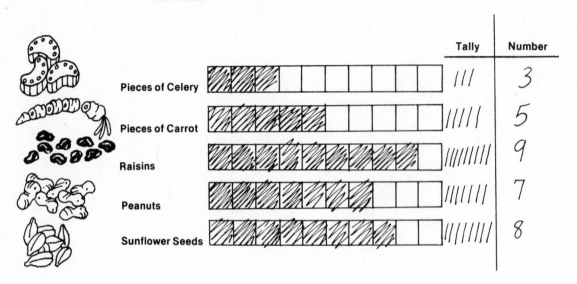

	Tally	Number
Pieces of Celery	///	3
Pieces of Carrot	//////	5
Raisins	/////////	9
Peanuts	///////	7
Sunflower Seeds	////////	8

Once this is done, give them Work Sheet 1-F3. They are to graph the number of objects specified and then record the number next to the representation.

Concept G: Seriation

Activity 1-G1.
(concrete)

•*Materials*   One small package of M & M's per student, six paper strips (black, brown, yellow, green, orange, and white) marked in squares, glue, scissors.

•*Procedure*   Begin the activity by asking math questions kids care about: "Do all these packages have the same number of M & M's?" "How many different colors are there in a bag?" "Are there the same number of each color?" "Which color do you think has the most?" *"How could you find out?"*

Name _____

Object											Number

Fingers on One Hand

Pieces of Clothing

Your Brothers and Sisters

Your Pets

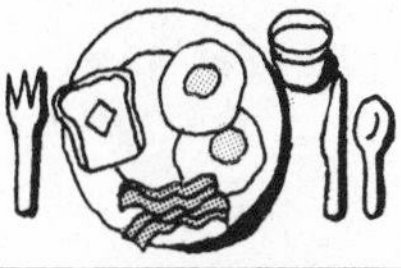

Meals You Eat in One Day

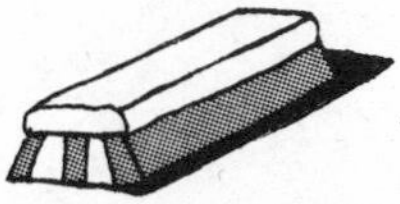

Board Erasers

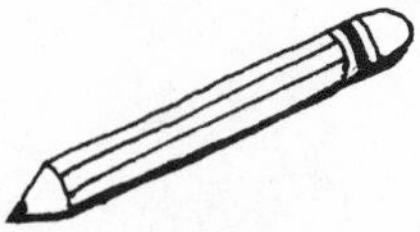

Pencils in Your Desk

Adults in the Room

From *Mathmatters*, copyright © 1978 by Goodyear Publishing Company, Inc.

Have the students open their bags of M & M's and sort them by color. They will usually find five colors: dark brown, tan, orange, green, and yellow. Let them compare among themselves to see who has the most of each color. Next have students glue each M & M on like-colored strips, one to a square.

When done, their collection may look like this:

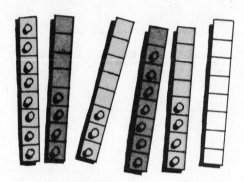

The white strip is glued onto the left side of a large piece of construction paper. This strip represents zero M & M's. Next to the white strip, the students glue the colored strip with the next fewest candies.

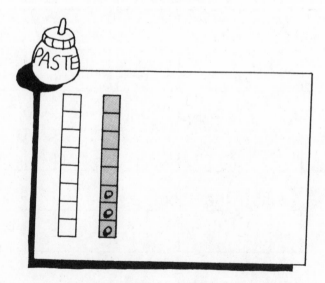

Continue this procedure until all six paper strips are glued in place.

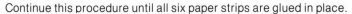

(An additional quantity of M & M's designated "for eating" may be necessary in order to ensure that enough of the candies are properly affixed to the colored strips.)

•*Materials*   M & M graphs from Activity 1-G1, graph paper, crayons.

•***Procedure***   Ask students how, if they were to "eat their graphs," they could remember who had the most of each color, or who had the most altogether. Suggest making a record as in previous activities. Students can record the results of their M & M graphs by using the same-color crayon as M & M to fill in the appropriate number of squares on the graph paper.

Note: The grid size should be the same size as the squares on the M & M strips.

Activity 1-G2.
(representational)

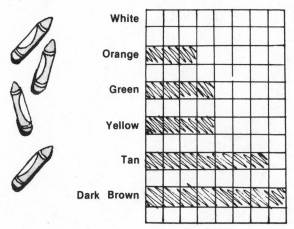

Activity 1-G3.
(symbolic)

•*Materials*   Unifix towers representing numbers one through nine (1–9), 3 × 5 cards, pencils. (Glitter and glue are optional.)

•***Procedure***   Have students "order" their Unifix towers in the same manner as they did the M & M strips in Activity 1-G1—i.e., smallest to largest.

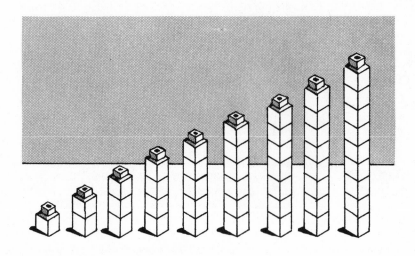

Place a 3 × 5 card by each tower and have students record the appropriate numerals.

If time permits, let students make these cards into "glitter numbers" by putting glue on the numerals and sprinkling with glitter. Distribute towers and numeral cards to nine students (card in one hand, tower in the other) and have them get themselves "in order" (one through nine). Pick another student with no card or tower and have him stand next to number one. Ask, "Who has more? Jason [holding number one] or Joshua [holding nothing]?" Then ask, "What do we call the tower Joshua is holding?" Draw a zero on a card and give it to Joshua. Have the individual students count out loud, in order, each saying his or her own number. Repeat this activity with different children until all the students have held all the towers and corresponding cards.

Activity 1-G4.
(symbolic)

•*Materials*   Paper, pencils, Work Sheet 1-G4.

•***Procedure***   Students can improve their ordering and counting skills by participating in daily routines. Student helpers count lunch buyers, milk buyers, and "nothing buyers" and take attendance. Class charts are kept of how often certain students use balls at recess, don't eat a snack, etc. Students who keep track of information that serves a useful purpose in classroom management will become more aware of activities taking place around them even as they are acquiring extensive practice in counting, recording numerals, and reading graphs.

Milk Buyers

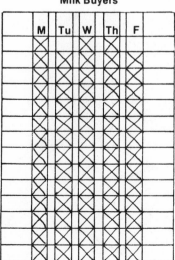

Lunch Buyers

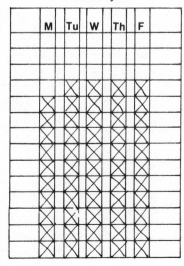

Nothing Buyers

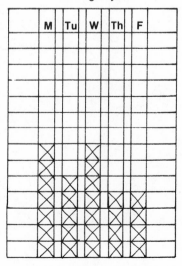

Choose a class recorder to mark off squares every time a student takes a milk or a lunch, etc. At the end of the week, a symbolic graph is made by each child (Work Sheet 1-G4).

	MON	TUES	WED	THURS	FRI
Milk	15	14	15	15	13
Lunch	10	10	11	11	10
Nothing	5	5	5	5	3

Name_____

	Mon	Tues	Weds	Thurs	Fri
Milk Buyers					
Lunch Buyers					
Nothing Buyers					

Milk Buyers						**Lunch Buyers**						**Nothing Buyers**				
	M	T	W	Th	F		M	T	W	Th	F		M	T	W	Th	F
15						15						15					
14						14						14					
13						13						13					
12						12						12					
11						11						11					
10						10						10					
9						9						9					
8						8						8					
7						7						7					
6						6						6					
5						5						5					
4						4						4					
3						3						3					
2						2						2					
1						1						1					

Addition and Subtraction

Children come into daily contact with addition and subtraction situations. In the concrete realm of a child's experience, it quickly becomes evident that when something is taken away (i.e., subtracted) one inevitably has less than he started with, and that when something is given, one will find he has more than he did when he started. These already familiar subtraction and addition situations can be staged in the classroom, utilizing objects the child can touch and manipulate. Prior to acquiring an abstract understanding of these basic concepts, however, a child must have the ability to visualize a set in relation to its parts. This readiness skill, called *set inclusion,* is discussed in detail in Appendix II.

A model consistent with this prerequisite understanding involves the use of Unifix cubes (see Appendix III). For example, by joining a red and blue tower together and then building an equivalent tower of a third color, it is possible to visualize the two original sets and the final solution.

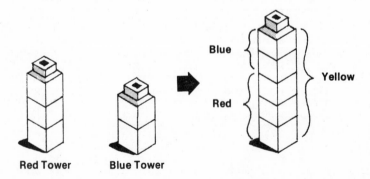

Red Tower   **Blue Tower**

Blue

Red

Yellow

After a child is comfortable with this process and becomes familiar with place-value notation, multiple-digit addition and subtraction algorithms can be developed. Base-ten materials should be introduced at this time. Student-constructed learning aids consisting of single tiles, tile strips (ten tiles glued to a strip of cardboard), and rafts (ten strips glued onto squares of cardboard) are excellent tools.

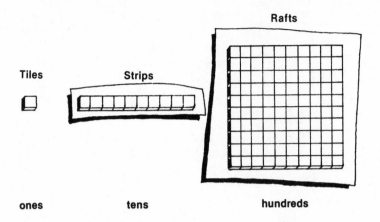

Rafts

Tiles   Strips

ones   tens   hundreds

Tile-strip materials in conjunction with a cardboard organizer make effective models of addition operations. Various tile pieces must be placed in the appropriate columns.

Addition Organizer

Rafts	Strips	Tiles
Hundreds	Tens	Ones

A problem can be posed as follows:

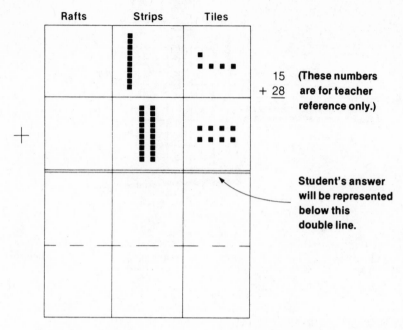

15   (These numbers
+ 28   are for teacher
       reference only.)

Student's answer
will be represented
below this
double line.

Instruct students to work from the right, combining the ones first. When tiles combine to make more than ten ones, they must be regrouped (adding a new tile strip to the tens column) and those remaining brought down to the answer spot.

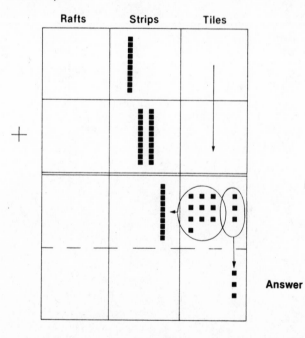

Answer

Next, the tens columns are combined.

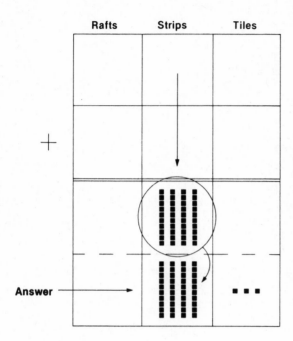

Since in this case no regrouping is required, the strips need only be brought down to complete the answer.

Children find this model very helpful when learning to carry out the regrouping process associated with addition. They will find that the transition to symbolic notation as introduced by the activities described in this section is much easier after assimilating concrete experiences such as those offered by the tile organizer.

The subtraction organizer differs from the addition organizer chiefly because of the subtrahend. The bottom number in the subtraction problem

$$\begin{array}{r} 9\ \textbf{Apples} \\ -\ 6\ \textbf{Apples} \end{array}$$

does not represent six additional apples; it indicates how many of the original nine apples must be taken away. The model below is useful in that the subtrahend is represented by "friends" to whom one each of the original quantity of tiles must be distributed.

Subtraction Organizer

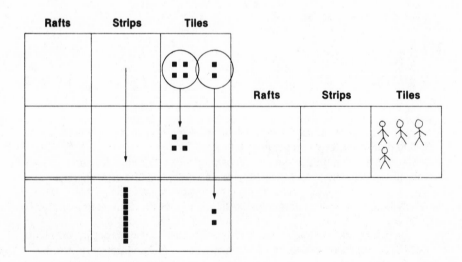

Each friend is given one tile, and the remainder is brought down to the bottom.

This procedure can be extended to the operation of subtraction problems that involve regrouping.

It is suggested that multidigit addition and subtraction problems that call for regrouping should be taught at the same time as problems that don't require regrouping. This facilitates true understanding of the importance of place value in the manipulation of numbers. Regrouping and nonregrouping problems do not represent separate operations and should not be taught as such. By utilizing manipulative materials to model these algorithms, regrouping becomes a natural and readily understood component of addition and subtraction.

Concept A: Place Value

•*Materials*   Tiles, tile strips, large numbers of objects to count.

•**Procedure**   Divide students into pairs, giving one partner a bag of ten individual tiles and the other a bag containing a number of tile strips. Ask them to count a particular group of objects, for example, the number of kickballs in the schoolyard? One student takes a single tile from his bag each time he comes upon a kickball. When that student "runs out" of tiles—i.e., after ten single tiles have been removed—those tiles are returned to the ones bag while the partner takes a tile strip from the tens bag. They continue counting objects in this manner, trading ten tiles for a tile strip, until they have counted all the objects. When the tallied tiles and tile strips are returned to the classroom, the result may look like this:

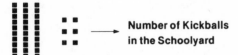

**Number of Kickballs
in the Schoolyard**

Other children should be asked to "name" this number: "How many kickballs were found?" Allow students to count the tiles on each tile strip one by one until they no longer find it necessary in order to arrive at the total number. Have partners switch roles and repeat the activity.

•*Materials*   Fingers, objects to count.

•**Procedure**   Divide students into pairs, again asking them to count large numbers of objects outside of the classroom. This time, in place of tiles, they are to use only their fingers as a means of record keeping. One student, Joshua, uses his fingers to count the objects, while another, Sarah, uses hers to keep track of the number of times Joshua goes through all his fingers. This is similar to the trading-in process of Activity 2-A1, but this time *one* of Sarah's fingers represents *ten* objects. The results the students bring back into the classroom may look like this:

Activity 2-A1.
(concrete)

Activity 2-A2.
*(concrete/
representational)*

Number of Kickballs in the Schoolyard

It now becomes important to talk about the relative worth of Sarah's and Joshua's fingers. Students are asked how many objects one of Sarah's fingers represents. If they appear to be unsure of this concept, have the pair go through an actual counting of ten in front of the entire group with Sarah raising one finger only after Joshua has used all ten of his. Students soon realize that Sarah's fingers are worth ten of Joshua's and therefore represent ten objects.

Give each pair one work sheet (like the one below) on which to record their findings pictorially, writing the total number of objects counted underneath the fingers drawn on their work sheets.

To emphasize the importance of position, have the same pairs repeat the exercise with roles reversed. The resulting graph would then have Joshua's fingers on the left and Sarah's on the right. Soon students will realize that the right column represents ones and the left column tens.

Activity 2-A3.
*(representational/
symbolic)*

•*Materials*   Objects to count, pencils, Work Sheet 2-A3.

•*Procedure*   As in Activity 2-A2, students count objects using their fingers. Upon reentering the room, each pair is given Work Sheet 2-A3, which presents problems that look like this (the objects to be counted will vary):

Students are then asked to record symbolically, in the appropriate positions, the number of fingers they have raised.

Ask the class, "How many flowers did Joshua and Sarah count?" Twenty-three! Then request that they validate their answer by counting through their own fingers the indicated number of times.

(2) Two Times Through	Three Fingers
Two Tens	**Three Ones**

Names _____

_____

Record your findings.

Example:

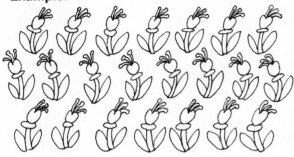 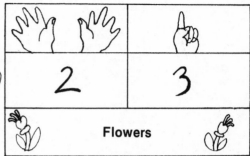

1. Count the number of classrooms at your school.

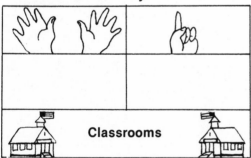

2. How many people at your school wear glasses?

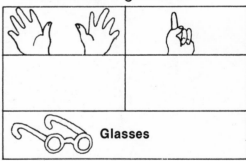

3. How many dogs are owned by people at your school?

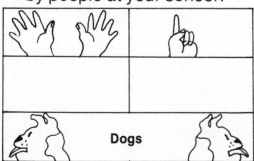

4. How many toes are sitting at your table?

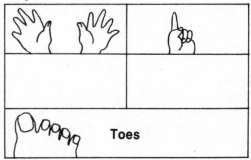

Concept B: Place Value—Representational

Activity 2-B1.
(concrete)

•*Materials*   Tiles, tile strips.

•***Procedure***   Large quantities of tiles and tile strips are placed before a group of students. The teacher or leader asks the group to show a specific number—e.g., 18— as quickly as possible. Some students, if not all of them, will rapidly count out eighteen individual tiles. Repeat this activity naming larger and larger two-digit numbers and hence making it increasingly tedious to count out the entire number with single tiles. At some point during this process, students will pick up a tile strip instead of ten individual tiles. Once this happens, stop and talk about the "best way" to pick up ten tiles. Ask which is quicker, picking up ten single tiles or one tile strip. Students will soon understand the efficiency of selecting a tile strip instead of ten single tiles. Now ask them to pick up eighteen tiles the "best way." Continue to ask students to show groups of tiles under twenty until they are comfortably and consistently picking up a strip to represent ten.

When asked the "best way" to show 24 (or any two-digit number greater than 20), students may tend to select only one strip and count the remainder in single tiles. If they don't progress on their own to picking up a tile strip for every group of ten, the teacher should talk about that possibility and arrange an example, asking, "Is mine the same number of tiles as yours? If so, which way is quicker?"

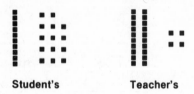

Student's   **Teacher's**

Continue this activity until students are consistently picking up tile strips for every group of ten.

Activity 2-B2.
*(concrete/
representational)*

•*Materials*   Tiles, tile strips, pencils, Record Sheet 2-B3.

Note: For this activity, it is necessary to develop a set of notations that represent tiles, such that students may have a "shorthand" for recording concrete problems. Any system may be developed, though the following method has proved useful:

Represents a Single Tile: ■

Represents a Tile Strip: ■■■■■■■■■■

Represents a Raft of Tile Strips:

•***Procedure*** Give each student access to a pile of tiles and tile strips and ask questions similar to those asked in Activity 2-B1. Let students review the "best way" of picking up numbers of tiles until they seem comfortable selecting a tile strip for all groups of ten.

Next, ask the children to show you a specific number—32, perhaps. After they have each found the "best way"—i.e., three tile strips and two single tiles—ask them to record the configuration using the representational notation developed.

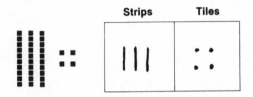

Strips	Tiles
|||	:: :

Continue this procedure with increasingly larger numbers. As they become familiar with the notation, students will want to go directly to the representational stage. This progression should be encouraged. Remove the tiles and tile strips when students no longer need them as a model, and continue to pose "best way" problems, asking students to use only the shorthand notation.

Teacher says: **Students write:**

48

24 →

31

Name_____

Strips	Tiles	Strips	Tiles

•*Materials*   Pencils, tiles, tile strips, Record Sheet 2-B3.

•*Procedure*   Provide students with a work sheet on which to record their "best way" problems.

Activity 2-B3.
(representational/ symbolic)

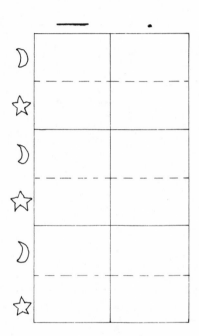

Call out numbers, asking students to record it in the "best way" (representational notation). These notations should be made in the column following the moon (or whatever symbol you prefer). Next, ask students to record the number of strips and tiles represented by each configuration. This notation should be made under in the row following the star.

First Step   ) | | | | : : :
                             : : :

Second Step ☆   4   6

Name_____

▬▬▬▬▬	●
🌙	
⭐	
🌙	
⭐	
🌙	
⭐	
🌙	
⭐	
🌙	
⭐	

Do this using many different numbers, always asking students to verbalize the number that appears in the star row.

Now prepare the same type of record sheet, but this time write the numeral in first.

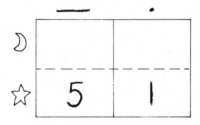

Ask students either to draw in the appropriate representational notation or to show you how many tiles and tile strips the symbolic notation 51 represents.

The preceding activities may easily be extended to include the hundreds place (a "hundred" is made by gluing ten tile strips to a piece of cardboard of the appropriate size). As mentioned previously, this piece is referred to as a "raft" and is represented notationally with a □. The teacher who wishes to include hundreds in activities 2-B1 through 2-B3 may call out numbers greater than 99 after students have proved themselves capable of consistently picking up tile strips for sets of ten, twenty, thirty, etc. The cards and papers may be modified to include hundreds as follows:

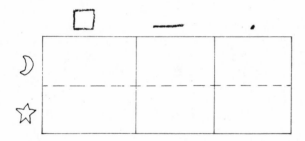

Concept C: Adding Small Numbers

•*Materials*   Unifix cubes in three colors.

Activity 2-C1.
(concrete)

•*Procedure*   Allow students to explore freely with Unifix cubes, building patterns and comparing towers. After an extensive period of exploration, construct two small towers from different-colored cubes.

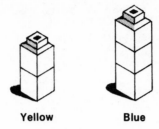

Yellow   Blue

Ask students to join these two towers and then to build a third tower the same height as the yellow and blue combination.

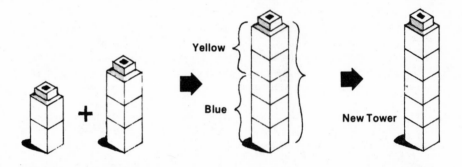

This process models the operation $2 + 3 = 5$. When separate colors are used to represent the addends (2 and 3), all three numbers in the problem (2, 3, and 5) are rendered visible. In models showing the union of sets of identical objects, the original numbers are much harder to distinguish once the sum has been obtained.

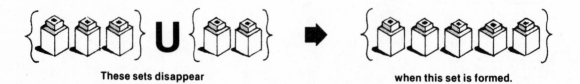

These sets disappear   when this set is formed.

Have students build pairs of towers which are then given to another student to join. (These problem situations should be limited to sums less than or equal to ten.) Though some students will readily use number names when joining towers do not require that all students do so.

•*Materials*   Unifix cubes, crayons, Graph Paper 2-C2.

•***Procedure***   Ask students to join Unifix towers as in Activity 2-C1, giving them graph paper and appropriately colored crayons with which to keep a record of their activities. They must color one square for each Unifix cube in the two original towers (two columns) and then color a third column representing their union.

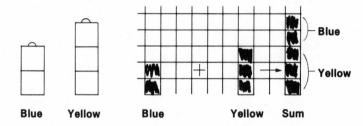

Blue   Yellow   Blue   Yellow   Sum

After students have had extensive experience using the graph paper as a recording tool, the teacher may eliminate the Unifix model. Have students create problems on the graph paper. For example, ask the children to color two towers, exchange papers, and solve each other's "problem."

If students have difficulty conceptualizing the sum of the graph towers, encourage them to cut out and join them; the operation then becomes even more concretely visible.

•*Materials*   Graph-paper problems, index cards, pencils, Unifix cubes.

•***Procedure***   Create addition problems on graph paper similar to those in Activity 2-C2.

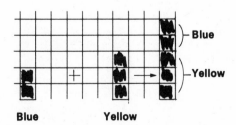

Blue   Yellow

After students successfully color in the sum, ask them to count the number of squares in each tower and to record those numbers on the 3 X 5 cards that have been marked with the appropriate operational symbols.

$$2 + 3 = 5$$

After the symbolic recordings have been made, collect the graph paper and ask the children to exchange their cards with partners. They must then validate the equations on the cards by building two Unifix towers, joining them, and checking the totals.

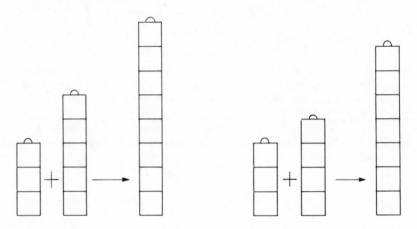

Give the students cards on which problems have been written. Ask them to solve the problems without resorting to the Unifix cubes. Once the answers have been written, however, have students use the cubes in order to validate their equations. (It is a good idea to hand out metal rings on which students may collect these fact cards as they master the information on them.)

Name_____

Concept D: Subtraction of Small Numbers

Activity 2-D1.
(concrete)

•*Materials*   Unifix cubes.

•***Procedure***   Stage a situational subtraction problem by seating groups of students around small piles of Unifix cubes. One student in each group holds all the cubes, and the other students each take one from him. Hence, if there are four students and a pile of five cubes, the leader will be left with a two-cube tower.

This example models the subtraction operation $5 - 3 = 2$. It can be extended to all subtraction situations by appropriate manipulation of the numbers of cubes and students.

Activity 2-D2.
(concrete/
representational)

•*Materials*   Unifix cubes, pencils, Subtraction Organizer 2-D2.

Subtraction Organizer 2-D2.

•***Procedure***   A number of cubes are placed in the top-left section of the subtraction organizer, the appropriate number of students are drawn in the middle-right section, and the subtraction problem is ready.

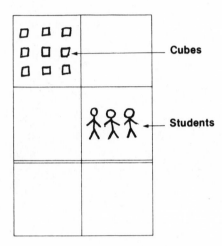

One cube for each student should then be removed from the top-left section and placed in the middle-left section (next to the drawing). The remaining cubes are brought down to the bottom section. These cubes constitute the answer.

1.
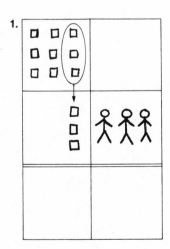

2.
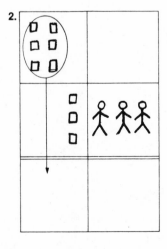

3.
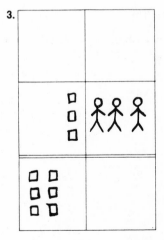

Repeat this activity, creating various subtraction situations.

Name

•*Materials*   Unifix cubes, subtraction organizer, pencils, Record Sheets 2-D3.

•*Procedure*   Students are given problems similar to those in Activity 2-D2. In conjunction with simply moving the cubes to their appropriate positions, however, they must now record the procedure both representationally (drawing squares) and symbolically (using numerals). Have students draw the Unifix arrangements and chart their movement as the subtraction operation is performed. Guide the operation by asking how many cubes there are to begin with, how many are taken away, and how many are left.

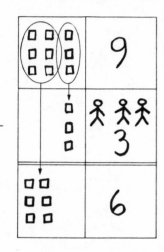

This dual system of recording provides students with a sense of the entire problem, even after the process has been completed. This is because they still have a record of the original quantity.

After extensive recording experience, students should be required to perform a verifying procedure. This time, instead of recording a concrete experience, they will be validating a symbolic manipulation. The same work sheets are used, but the symbols are given first. The students must recreate the problem with Unifix cubes, recording the answer symbolically.

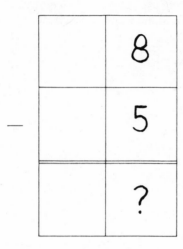 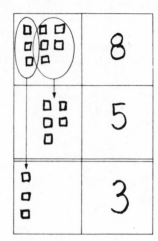

Students should now begin to find their answers *without* relying on Unifix cubes. At this point, ask them to validate (or check) their answers with the cubes.

Concept E: Addition Facts and the Commutative Property

Activity 2-E1.
*(concrete/
representational)*

•*Materials*   Bottle caps, recording cards (see below).

•*Procedure*   In order to help them define all possible pairs whose sum is a specific quantity, give students a number of bottle caps and a set of recording cards.

Bottle Caps

Recording Cards for Quantities of Five

Name_____

Example:

Your board

Your Record:

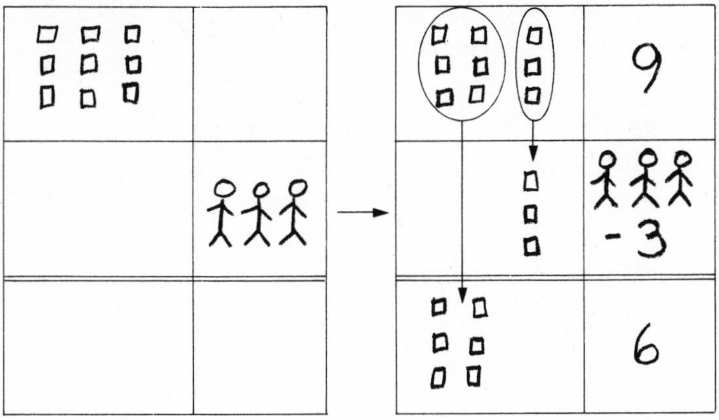

9

- 3

6

1.

2.

3.

4.

5.

6.

From *Mathmatters*, copyright © 1978 by Goodyear Publishing Company, Inc.

Ask students to toss the bottle caps and to record the various combinations of right-side-up and upside-down caps that result. Have them color in the number of upside-down bottle caps.

The other possible combinations of five bottle caps are

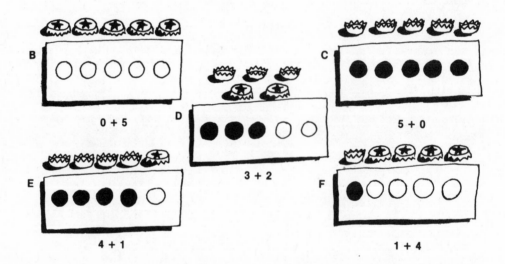

Students soon notice that something is similar on cards A and D, B and C, and E and F. They have discovered the commutative property for addition. To reinforce this concept, encourage students to examine specific pairs of situations and verbalize their observations.

To facilitate this exploration, the teacher might ask such questions as, "How are these two cards the same?" "How are they different?" "How many caps are there altogether on each card?" "How many are upside down?" "Right side up?" "Does this work for all numbers?"

The exercise should be repeated for all quantities of bottle caps, one through nine.

Activity 2-E2.
(representational/ symbolic)

•*Materials*   Bottle-cap cards from Activity 2-E1, pencils, blank addition tables, Work Sheet 2-E2.

•*Procedure*   Students are given completed recording cards and asked to write number sentences about them. (This could also be done with new recording cards, requiring that students again toss groups of bottle caps in order to obtain new combinations.)

Students must next take all their cards, group them by sum (all fives together, all threes together, etc.), and record the sums on an addition table. (Encourage the children to look for patterns like the diagonals illustrated below.)

Second Addend

First Addend	0	1	2	3	4	5	6	7	8	9
0						5		7		
1					5		7			
2				5		7				
3			5		7					
4		5		7						
5	5		7							
6		7								
7	7									
8										
9										

Sums

WORK SHEET 2-E2

Name____

ADDITION TABLE

Second Addend

First Addend

+	0	1	2	3	4	5	6	7	8	9
0										
1										
2										
3										
4										
5										
6										
7										
8										
9										

•*Materials*   Dice games.

•***Procedure***   Drill games constitute the most effective way to help students memorize the facts of addition. A pair of dice numbered zero (blank) through five gives every combination for sums zero through five and many for sums six to ten. Later, to extend this experience, you may have students label dice as they wish or design additional games. Here are some examples involving easily constructed game boards:

1. Each student rolls the dice and advances the number of spaces given by the sum.

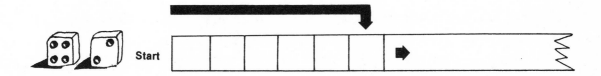

2. In an alternate approach to No. 1, the student moves to the next number on the game board that matches the sum of the dice.

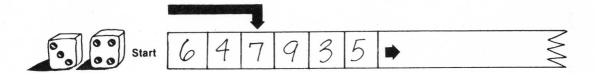

3. Eventually, games could involve matching alternate "names" (addition facts) for the same number.

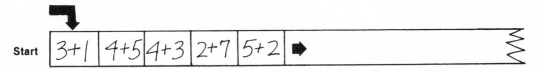

If a student rolled he would move to the first square (3 + 1), as it is the first position also equal to the sum of the dice.

Dominoes, and many card games (21, for example) are also excellent reinforcement activities for addition facts.

Concept F: Subtraction Facts

Activity 2-F1.
(concrete/ representational)

•*Materials*   Bottle caps, sets of recording cards for numbers one through nine (as devised for Activity 2-E1).

•*Procedure*   Give students a number of bottle caps, for tossing, and sets of cards on which to record the outcomes. After students make their tosses, instruct them to "take away," or subtract, all upside-down bottle caps. They record this procedure on their cards by crossing out the number of caps they remove.

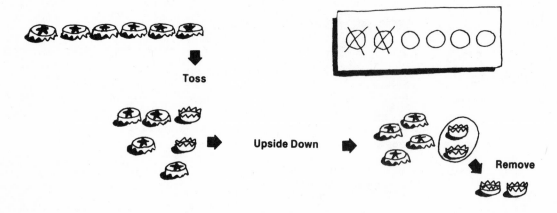

Toss

Upside Down

Remove

This is repeated for all subtraction facts one through nine.

Activity 2-F2.
(representational/ symbolic)

•*Materials*   Bottle caps, recording cards, pencils, Work Sheet 2-F2.

•*Procedure*   Students repeat Activity 2-F1, this time recording the process numerically (symbolically) as they proceed. If the caps were to land in this manner,

two would be taken away. This is shown on the card by crossing out two caps and by writing 5 – 2. The remaining caps are then counted and the symbolic record is completed: 5 – 2 = 3.

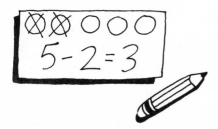

Give students a blank work sheet similar to the one below. Ask them to fill in the table using their recording cards as references.

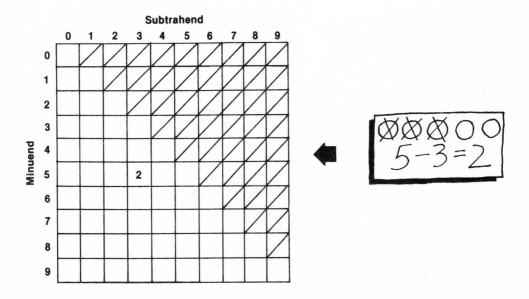

The fact that only one-half the table can be filled in should be explained. Asking questions like "Can you take three bottle caps away from only two?" or "If you had five pieces of candy, could you give me seven?" helps demonstrate why parts of the table must remain blank.

Name_____

SUBTRACTION TABLE

Subtrahend

	0	1	2	3	4	5	6	7	8	9
0										
1										
2										
3										
4										
5										
6										
7										
8										
9										

Minuend

• *Materials*   Dice games.

• **Procedure**   Develop games similar to the addition drills. This time, the two dice are rolled and the larger number placed in front of the smaller. The difference indicates the number of moves or the next number to move to. Games combining addition and subtraction should also be prepared.

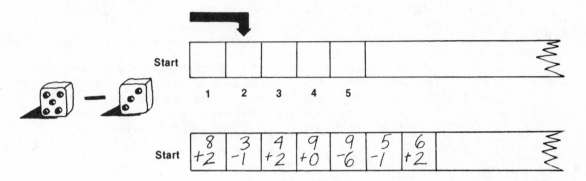

Aside from providing valuable practice, these games allow students to enjoy what might otherwise prove to be a dull period of reinforcement in the teaching of mathematics.

Concept G: Two-Place Addition with Regrouping

In most mathematics sequences, one generally finds two-place addition without regrouping introduced before and apart from problems that involve the regrouping process. However, these two types of problems involve only one process, namely, addition of multiple-place numbers. Children do not view adding twenty-two and thirteen pieces of candy as being different from adding twenty-two and nineteen pieces. Furthermore, when addition without regrouping is introduced separately, children fail to recognize the place-value relationship in two-digit numbers. The problem

   28
 + 41

becomes 8 + 1 and 2 + 4. (Ask a child which represents more in twenty-eight, the eight or the two.)

Because the concept of place value is lost when the two digits are thought of as separate entities, children understandably encounter difficulty when they must eventually learn to regroup. Suddenly, the two digits must be related in some manner and cannot be dealt with separately.

To avoid this confusion, two-digit addition with regrouping must be introduced simultaneously with nonregrouping situations. The concept should be presented in such a manner that both facets (regrouping and nonregrouping) are viewed as a natural and integral part of the process of addition.

Activity 2-G1.
(concrete)

•*Materials*   Tiles, tile strips, Work Sheet 2-G1.

•*Procedure*   Students are given boards and asked to work problems that are given to them verbally. Again, place values are represented on the board by columns for single tiles, strips of ten, and rafts of one hundred.

When asked, for example, to add seventeen and twenty-five, students first combine all the single tiles (ones) and move them to the answer block.

Students are then asked how many individual tiles there are in all and whether this is the "best way" (see Activity 2-B1) to show twelve. They should respond that the best way would be by means of a tile strip and two single tiles. At this, the teacher points out that students must therefore trade ten individual tiles for a tile strip and move the tile strip into the appropriate column.

| Rafts | Strips | Tiles |

The same process is then repeated for the tile strip column.

| Rafts | Strips | Tiles |

The resulting group of tile strips (including the one compiled from the tiles place) is examined to see whether it, too, is the "best way" to show forty. Since in this case forty is already represented correctly, the problem is completed and the answer is forty-two.

Here is how the sum 153 + 64 would be handled:

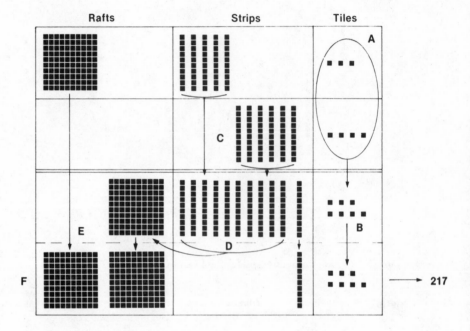

All the single tiles are combined (A) and then checked to see whether the sum is represented in the "best way" (B). In this instance, it is represented in the best way, so we leave it alone. Next all the tile strips are combined (C). This time we must change the tile-strip group to the "best way" (D) by trading ten strips for a raft of one hundred. The raft is placed in its column (E) and with the other raft is brought down to the answer block where they are again checked for the "best way." Thus, the answer (F) is obtained.

Activity 2-G2.
*(concrete/
representational)*

•*Materials*   Tiles, tile strips, addition organizer, pencils, Record Sheet 2-G2.

•*Procedure*   Once again, give students an addition problem to be solved by means of addition boards, tiles, and tile strips. Ask them to use our representational notation in order to record the problem-solving process. In this way they experience both a concrete situation,

Name

ADDITION ORGANIZER

Tile Rafts	Tile Strips	Tiles

Name_____

1.

Rafts	Strips	Tiles

2.

Rafts	Strips	Tiles

3.

Rafts	Strips	Tiles

4.

Rafts	Strips	Tiles

5.

Rafts	Strips	Tiles

6.

Rafts	Strips	Tiles

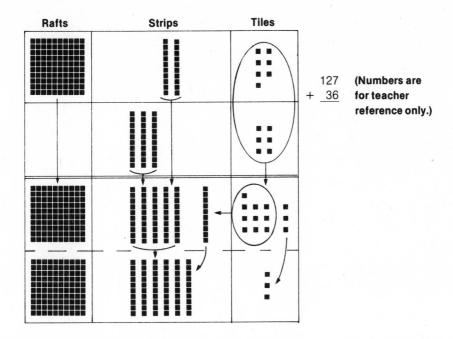

	127	(Numbers are
	+ 36	for teacher
		reference only.)

and the making of a representational record.

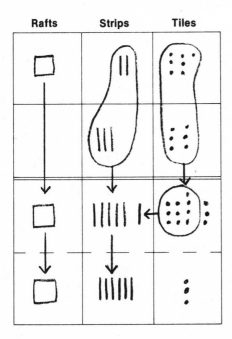

In contrast to the concrete model, representational notation allows the original addends to remain visible. After students have acquired extensive experience in using this notation as a recording process, the tile-strip model may be eliminated and all work done at the representational level.

Work sheets like the following may be developed (numerals are for teacher reference only; problems are given orally):

Rafts	Strips	Tiles

$\begin{array}{r} 25 \\ + 27 \\ \hline \end{array}$

Rafts	Strips	Tiles

$\begin{array}{r} 153 \\ + \ 65 \\ \hline \end{array}$

•*Materials*   Pencils, tiles, tile strips, Work sheets 2-G2 and 2-G3.

•***Procedure***   Students are given representational problems and asked to make a symbolic record of their transactions on Record Sheet 2-G2.

When students have become familiar with the mechanics of symbolic notation, the representational schema is eliminated and problems are handled in an entirely symbolic manner (Work Sheet 2-G3). After computing the answer, students should write the entire problem next to the chart.

Activity 2-G3.
(representational/ symbolic)

Rafts	Strips	Tiles
	‖‖‖ 6	• • • • • 5
	‖ 2	• • • • / • • • • 8
	(‖‖‖‖/) 8+1	(• • • • •) ← (13)
	‖‖‖‖‖ 9	• • • 3

	100s	10s	1s
		2	6
		9	2
		‖	8
	1	1	8

26
+ 92

118

Name_____

Example:

A.

Hundreds	Tens	Ones
	3	4
	2	8
	5	12
	6	2

+

$$\begin{array}{r} 34 \\ + 28 \\ \hline 62 \end{array}$$

1.

Hundreds	Tens	Ones
1	2	6
	9	2

+

2.

Hundreds	Tens	Ones
1	2	7
2	1	1

+

3.

Hundreds	Tens	Ones
5	2	9
	7	8

+

4.

Hundreds	Tens	Ones
2	9	0
3	7	8

+

5.

Hundreds	Tens	Ones
7	0	6
	9	8

+

From *Mathmatters*, copyright © 1978 by Goodyear Publishing Company, Inc.

Ask them to validate these symbolic manipulations using tiles and tile strips.

Rafts	Strips	Tiles

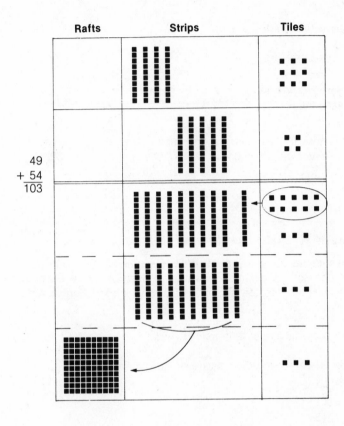

$$\begin{array}{r} 49 \\ +\ 54 \\ \hline 103 \end{array}$$

Students first complete the problems at the symbolic level, then validate their answers using concrete materials.

Activity 2-G4.
(symbolic)

•*Materials*   Pencils, Work Sheet 2-G3.

•**Procedure**   A fascinating phenomenon for children to explore, as well as a welcome alternative to the traditionally dull routine of drill and practice, is the palindrome, a word or number that reads the same forward and backward: pop, tot, toot, radar, 101, 2112, 23232, 111. Palindromes can also be complete sentences: Madam, I'm Adam.

A most interesting aspect of the numerical palindrome is the way in which it can be derived. Pick any number, reverse it, and add the two.

$$\begin{array}{r} 421 \\ +\ 124 \\ \hline 545 \end{array}$$

The result is a palindrome!

Sometimes it takes more than one step.

```
    273
  +  372
    645
  +  546      Reverse and Add
   1191
  + 1911      Reverse and Add
   3102
  + 2013      Reverse and Add
   5115      Palindrome
```

This will always work. You can use any number and eventually you will reach a palindrome! A calculator might be handy if you try the number 89.

Concept H: Subtraction with Regrouping

Note: When students are working with multiple-digit numbers, subtraction with and without regrouping are introduced simultaneously as two facets of the same concept that should not be separated (see the introduction to Activity 2-G1).

Activity 2-H1.
(concrete)

•*Materials*   Tiles, tile strips, subtraction boards.

•*Procedure*   Subtraction problems are set up in this manner:

Example 1.

**(Numbers are for
teacher reference only.)**

```
  22
-  8
```

Name_____

Find palindromes for these numbers.

Example:

```
    935
  + 539
   1474
  + 4741
   6215
  + 5126
  11321
 + 12311
  23632   Yeah!
```

1. 135

2. 435

3. 251

4. 291

5. 361

6. 497

The tiles in the far-right box represent the "friends" used when developing the concept of subtraction (see Activity 2-F2). This should be made evident to the students.

Ask students whether they have enough single tiles to give each friend one. After they respond negatively, ask them where they could possibly get more. Encourage them to exchange a tile strip for ten individual tiles, which are then placed in the appropriate position.

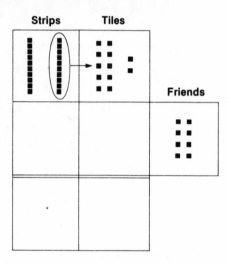

Now are there enough tiles for each friend to have one?
The process may now be completed.

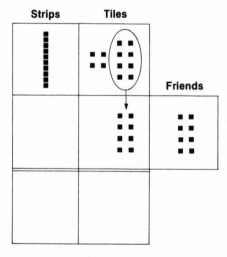

First, one tile for each friend is "taken away" from the original quantity. Next, the answer (first the ones place, then the tens) is brought down to its final position.

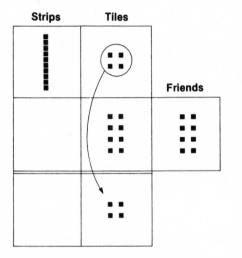 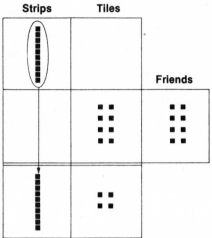

Example 2.

22
− 15

Step 1. Regroup tile strip to tiles place.

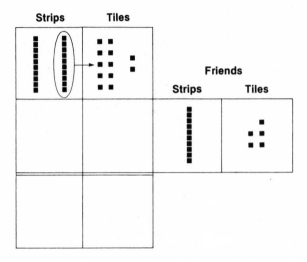

Step 2. Take away appropriate number of tiles (from the ones place) and bring the rest down to their final position.

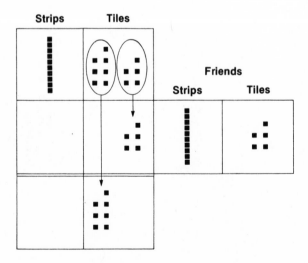

Step 3. Take away appropriate number of tile strips (from tens place) and bring any remaining strips down to the final-answer place (in this case, none).

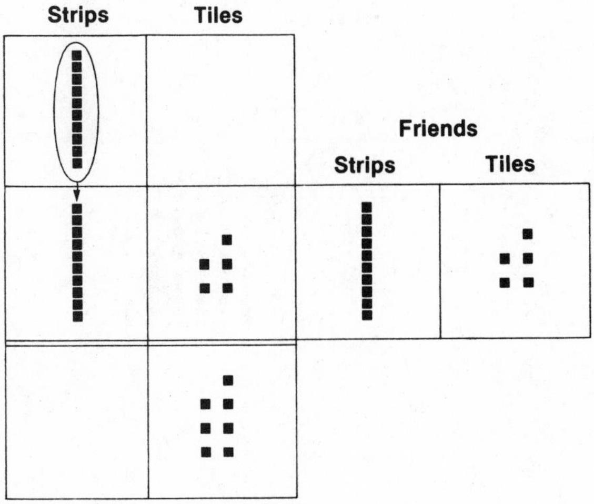

Strips   **Tiles**

Friends

Strips   **Tiles**

Example 3.

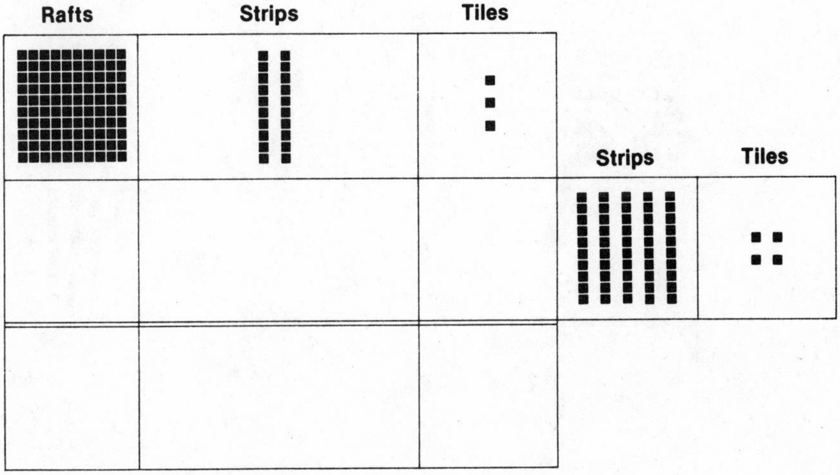

Rafts   **Strips**   **Tiles**

Strips   **Tiles**

123
− 54

Step 1. Since there aren't enough loose tiles, regroup one tile strip and place tiles in ones column.

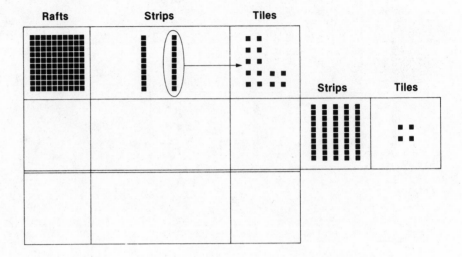

Step 2. Subtract appropriate number of tiles and bring down remainder.

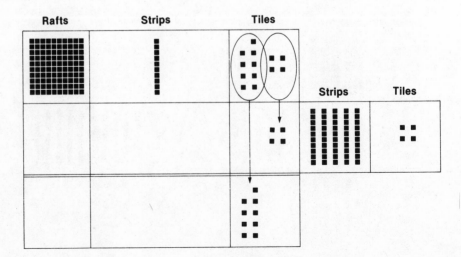

Step 3. Since there aren't enough tile strips, regroup one raft and place in tile-strip column.

Step 4. Subtract appropriate number of tile strips and bring down remainder.

Activity 2-H2.
(concrete/ representational)

• *Materials*   Tiles, tile strips, Record Sheet 2-H2.

• **Procedure**   Repeat Activity 2-H1, but this time have students record their process using representational notation. Develop work sheets with the boards already drawn on them, i.e.,

Rafts	Strips	Tiles

		Friends	
	Rafts	Strips	Tiles

For the problem 34 – 16, the concrete situation would look like this:

and the representational record would look like this:

Rafts	Strips	Tiles
	|||	:: :

Strips	Tiles
		:: : :

Rafts	Strips	Tiles

First regroup tile strip to tiles place.

Rafts	Strips	Tiles

Strips	Tiles

Rafts	Strips	Tiles

Strips	Tiles

Next, subtract appropriate number of tiles and bring the answer down to the ones place.

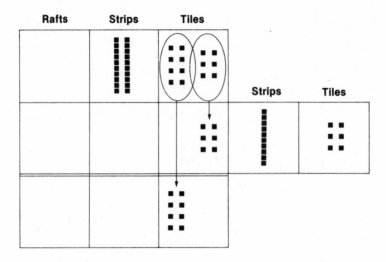

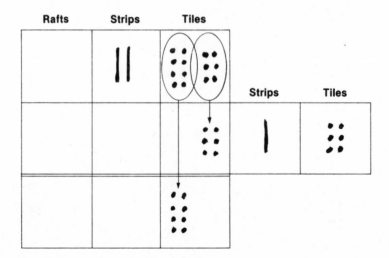

Finally, subtract the appropriate number of tile strips and bring the remaining answer down to the tens place. The problem has now been solved.

RECORD SHEET 2-H2 SUBTRACTION

Name ____

Rafts	Strips	Tiles

Friends

Rafts	Strips	Tiles

Rafts	Strips	Tiles

Friends

Rafts	Strips	Tiles

Rafts	Strips	Tiles

Friends

Rafts	Strips	Tiles

Rafts	Strips	Tiles

Rafts	Strips	Tiles

Rafts	Strips	Tiles

Rafts	Strips	Tiles

Rafts	Strips	Tiles

Rafts	Strips	Tiles

Activity 2-H3.
(representational/symbolic)

•*Materials* Paper, tiles, tile strips, Record Sheet 2-H2.

•***Procedure*** To familiarize students with symbolic notation for subtraction, have them use numerals to record their representational process on a separate sheet of paper.

Original Problem:

Record:

$$\begin{array}{r} 3\ \ 5 \\ -\,1\ \ 9 \\ \hline \end{array}$$

Regroup:

Record:

$$\begin{array}{r} 2\ \ \ \ \ \\ \not{3}\ \ 15 \\ -\,1\ \ \ 9 \\ \hline \end{array}$$

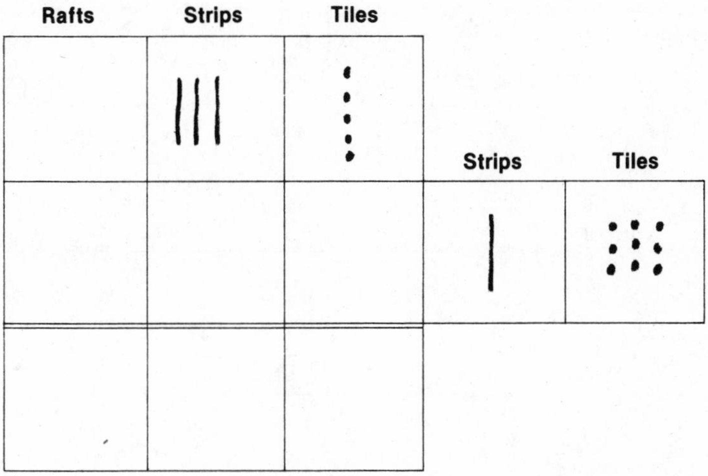

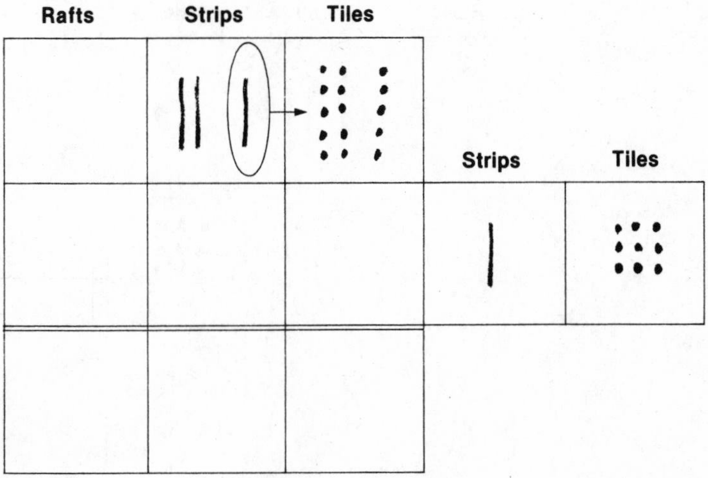

Subtract and bring down answer (ones column).

Subtract:

Record:

$$
\begin{array}{r}
2 \\
\cancel{3}15 \\
-\ 1\ 9 \\
\hline
6
\end{array}
$$

Subtract and bring down answer (tens column).

Subtract:

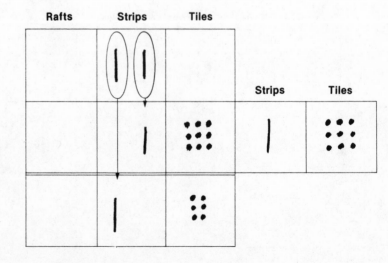

Record:

$$
\begin{array}{r}
2 \\
\cancel{3}15 \\
-\ 1\ 9 \\
\hline
1\ 6
\end{array}
$$

After students have become familiar with the mechanics of symbolic notation, provide them with problems to be solved entirely at the symbolic level. Ask
them to validate their answers by repeating the process with concrete
materials or representational notation. For example, the problem 35 – 16 is
given and the student finds an answer (19) at the symbolic level. He is then
asked to validate his answer using tiles and tile strips. He sets up the problem,

Strips	Tiles

Strips	Tiles

regroups,

Strips	Tiles

Strips	Tiles

subtracts ones and brings down the answer,

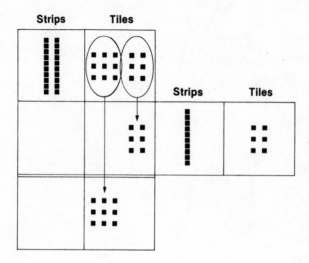

subtracts tens and brings down the answer.

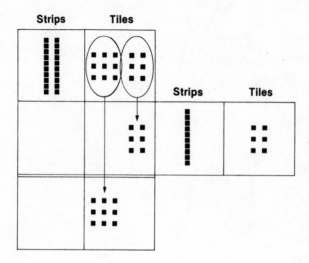

The final answer is

i.e., 19—right!

•*Materials*   Pencils, Work Sheet 2-H4.

•***Procedure***   Here is an interesting number property which can be used to spark students' interest in subtraction drills. Take any three-digit number (first and last digits must be different), reverse it, and subtract the smallest of the two from the largest. Next, reverse the difference and add. The answer will always be 1,089!

```
      452
  −   254
      198
  +   891
    1,089
```

Here's another example:

```
                        423
                   −    324  Reverse and Subtract
                        099
(In these cases you must include the zero.)  +    990  Reverse and Add
                      1,089  Eureka!!!
```

This exercise provides a self-checking mechanism for a student's subtraction. If his final sum adds up to 1,089, he knows that his subtraction was correct; if he gets something else, he will know something went wrong.

Name_____

Find the magic number.

Examples:	A.	421	B.	629
Reverse and Subtract		$-\underline{124}$		926
		297		$-\underline{629}$
Reverse and Add		$+\underline{792}$		297
Right!!		1,089		$+\underline{792}$
Right!!!				1,089

1. 391

2. 984

3. 423

4. 738

5. 667

Extra-Tough Puzzler   Why does this work?

Notes for Topic 2

Multiplication

One simple approach to multiplication is a direct outgrowth from experience with counting and addition. In order to save time, students may automatically begin to count by twos or threes. They may already have posed themselves such problems as, "How many wheels are there on three buses with six wheels apiece?" This initial experience with multiplication is based on repeated addition, and it is here that our activities begin on a concrete level. As addition begins to become unwieldy (adding forty-seven nineteens would be a large pain!) the array model introduced below provides a shortcut for counting. It imposes an easily manipulated visual pattern by rearranging numbers into manageable chunks. Within this framework, and through the successive short-cuts of representational and symbolic notation, students will find that they can manage large numbers. Look, for example, at 18 × 24.

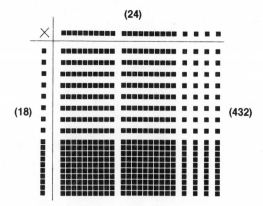

This arrangement offers a neat alternative to the laying out and adding up of eighteen twenty-fours. In time, students will find drawing pictures using our representational notation an easier alternative to laying out the concrete materials.

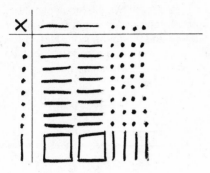

The final shortcut is to use symbolic (numerical) notation to record problems.

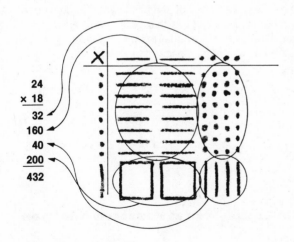

Notice how the various sections of the array represent the subproducts that comprise the multiplication procedure: 8 × 4, 8 × 20, 10 × 4, and 10 × 20.

In this section, we present two algorithms for two-digit multiplication. It is important to note that they are truly equivalent. In Algorithm A, the four component multiplication problems are worked and the four subproducts added. In Algorithm B, the first two subproducts are regrouped and added together, the next two are regrouped and added, and then the two partial products are added.

```
A.    24          B.    24
    × 18              × 18
      32               192
     160               240
      40               432
     200
     432
```

In each case, four mini-multiplication problems are worked and the four products added. Algorithm A follows directly from the concrete and representational models and leaves the subtotals visible. The multiplication and addition processes remain discrete. Though this method uses slightly more paper, it nevertheless seems to be somewhat simpler and less error prone. Algorithm B, however, is the method most of us have learned. If the benefits of uniformity seem to you to outweigh the advantages of simplicity, your students can later be taught to use Algorithm B, but we leave that choice and the approach to bringing about that transition to the individual teacher. (See Appendix 1 for a discussion of readiness diagnosis for multiplication.)

Concept A: Multiplication as Repeated Addition

Activity 3-A1.
(concrete)

• *Materials*   Cuisenaire rods.

• *Procedure*   Have the students make trains out of the same-colored rods.

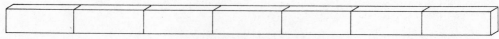

Seven Light Green Rods

Measuring the length of the train with orange rods and determining the number of whites left over is an easy means of comparing train length.

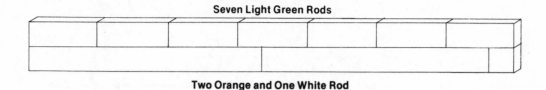

Seven Light Green Rods

Two Orange and One White Rod

Four yellow rods would be measured as follows:

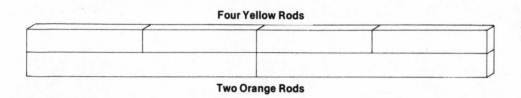

Four Yellow Rods

Two Orange Rods

Encourage students to create their own problems and compare the lengths of trains with equivalent orange-and-white combinations.

•*Materials* Centimeter graph paper, crayons, Work Sheet 3-A2.

•***Procedure*** Have students represent the rod trains using centimeter graph paper and crayons.

Activity 3-A2.
(representational)

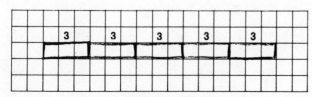

Five Light Green Rods

Ask them to determine the number of orange rods (tens) and white rods (ones) necessary to create a train of equal length.

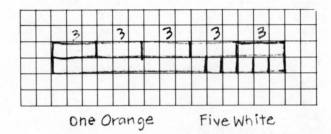

One Orange   Five White

Encourage students to record the results using symbolic notation, as in the figure above. Some may discover that the number of orange and white rods can be determined by adding five threes.

Five Threes =>   3 + 3 + 3 + 3 + 3 = 15 =>   One Orange Rod and Five White Rods

Activity 3-A3.
(symbolic)

•*Materials* Graph paper, Cuisenaire rods, paper, pencils, Work Sheet 3-A3.

•*Procedure* Provide students with problems similar to those below and encourage them to validate their results using either rods or graph-paper representations.

    Example 1:   Four Sixes 4 × 6 = 6 + 6 + 6 + 6 = 24
    Two Orange and Four White Rods

    Example 2:   Five Sevens 5 × 7 = 7 + 7 + 7 + 7 + 7 = 35
    Three Orange and Five White Rods

Encourage students to create their own problems and validate them with rods or sketches.

Name_____

For each problem, lay the correct number of colored rods
beside the line of squares and color the squares to match.

5 Light Green

Next find how many orange and white rods fit in this space.
Color the next row to match

L	I	G	H	T		G	R	E	E	N							
		O	R	A	N	G	E		W	H	I	T	E				

1. 4 Yellow
Orange + White

2. 3 Dark Green
Orange + White

3. 5 Purple
Orange + White

4. 2 Blue
Orange + White

5. 2 Brown
Orange + White

6. 2 Black
Orange + White

From *Mathmatters*, copyright © 1978 by Goodyear Publishing Company, Inc.

Name_____

How many orange and white rods are needed to equal each train?

You may use rods to help solve these problems.

$6 + 6 + 6 + 6$
$20 + 4 = 24$

$7 + 7 + 7 + 7$
$= |$
$+$

1. 4 Sixes

2. 4 Sevens

3. 2 Nines

4. 4 Eights

5. 6 Fours

6. 6 Fives

7. 8 Threes

8. 5 Twos

9. 3 Nines

From *Mathmatters*, copyright © 1978 by Goodyear Publishing Company, Inc.

Concept B: The Array Definition of Multiplication
(Multiplication Facts)

•*Materials*   Tiles, tile strips.

•*Procedure*   Students use loose tiles to build arrays that represent the repeated addition model for multiplication presented under Concept A. This is how students would represent the problem 4 × 5.

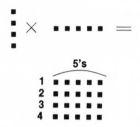

This example can be verified by counting each and every tile or by counting the tiles by fives ("Five, ten, fifteen, twenty"). Another method for determining the total number of tiles, one that eliminates the need for counting, is to trade loose tiles for tile strips.

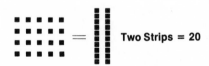

The students should do several problems of this type, trading tiles for strips as necessary. Use only single-digit factors for this activity.

•*Materials*   Tiles, tile strips, paper, pencils, Work Sheet 3-B2.

•*Procedure*   The representational notation used in Section II and pictured below will be utilized in several activities throughout the rest of the book. This representational notation is a significant step toward symbolic notation.

The figures in the center column of the table below "represent" the actual tile rafts, strips, and units, but can easily be written on paper. Their purpose is to provide a bridge between the concrete and symbolic representations of a concept.

Concrete	Representational	Symbolic
▪	●	|
(strip)	|	10
(raft)	▢	100

During this activity, students should be encouraged to use the representational notation. Eventually they will choose to use it, since it is more convenient for large problems.

Have the students solve problems such as the following:

Example 1.

$$: \times \cdots = ? $$

$$ :::: = \|\| \quad 4 \times 5 = 20 $$

Example 2.

$$: \times \cdots = ? $$

$$ ::: = \|\| : \quad 6 \times 4 = 24 $$

A record of all combinations (1 × 1 through 9 × 9) should be kept on a table similar to Work Sheet 3-B2.

×	1	2	3	4	5	6	7	8	9
1									
2									
3									
4				20					
5									
6			24						
7									
8									
9									

Discovering and using patterns (e.g. 4 × 5 = 20 =>5 × 4 = 20) should be encouraged. Once the whole table has been filled and validated, it should be kept for future use and eventually committed to memory.

•*Materials* Multiplication charts with several numbers missing (from 3-B2) and Worksheet 3-B3.

•*Procedure* Multiplication charts similar to the ones below are given to each student to be completed. Discovering and using patterns should be encouraged. Have the students make up tables to be completed by a partner.

Activity 3-B3.
(symbolic)

×	1	2	3	4	5	6	7	8	9
1	1								9
2	2	4							
3	3	6	9						
4	4	8	12	16					
5		10	15	20					
6			18	24					
7			28						
8									
9									81

×	1	3	5	7	9	2	4	6	8
1	1					2			8
3	3	9	15			6	12		24
5	5	15	25			10	20		40
7	7	21							
9									
2	2	6	10						
4	4	12	20						
6									
8	8	24	40						64

Name_____

Solve these multiplication problems. Use tile strips if you need help.

Example: $\vdots$ × ····· = [⁞⁞⁞⁞⁞] = ‖ = <u>20</u>

1. ⁞ × ···· = ⁞⁞⁞⁞ = ___ = _____

2. ⁞ × ········ = ___ = ___ = _____

3. ⁞ × ··· = ___ = ___ = _____

4. ⁞ × ····· = ___ = ___ = _____

5. ⁞ × ········· = ___ = ___ = _____

6. ⁞ × ········ = ___ = ___ = _____

Now make up your own problems.

× ___ = ___ = ___ ___

× ___ = ___ = ___ ___

× ___ = ___ = ___ ___

× ___ = ___ = ___ ___

× ___ = ___ = ___ ___

× ___ = ___ = ___ ___

Record all your answers on this times table.

×	1	2	3	4	5	6	7	8	9
1									
2									
3									
4					20				
5									
6									
7									
8									
9									

Name_____

Use tile strips to help fill in the chart. Look for patterns. How many squares can you fill in without using your tile strips?

×	1	2	3	4	5	6	7	8	9
1	1								
2	2	4							
3	3	6	9						
4	4	8	12	16					
5		10	15	20					
6				24					
7									
8									
9									81

Now see if you can figure out a way to fill in this table. (It *is* possible.)

×	3			2			7		
				4				16	18
3				18					
		21					70		
			16	24	4	28			
			40					64	
		27							81
				10					45
1				6	1				9

From *Mathmatters*, copyright © 1978 by Goodyear Publishing Company, Inc.

Once students have had extensive experience with multiplication facts and are attempting to commit them to memory, encourage the children to determine how many facts they *do* know. Full utilization of the commutative property by each student is prerequisite to memorizing the table. It should be pointed out that when a child is diagnosed as "not knowing the multiplication facts," what we really mean is that he doesn't know eight or ten of them! Out of the eighty-one facts of multiplication, most 10 to 11 year old children know at least seventy! The task of *learning* multiplication facts seems somewhat less formidable when viewed in this light.

Concept C: Multiplication of a Two-Digit by a One-Digit Number

Activity 3-C1.
(concrete)

•*Materials*   Single tiles, tile strips, rafts, yarn.

•*Procedure*   Give your students the following problem and have them solve it with tile materials: "How many tiles are there in eight rows of fourteen tiles?"

This problem can be recorded by using eight tiles to represent the number of rows and fourteen tiles (one tile strip and four loose tiles) to represent the number of tiles in each row.

To keep track of the problem, students now begin working within a yarn organizer (this activity should be done on the floor).

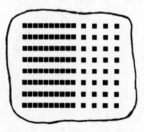

There will be a need to do a great deal of regrouping within the loop, so much so that the structure of the original problem may be lost. It is therefore wise to take on the convention of recording the problem outside the loop.

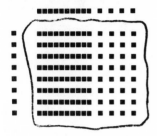

The answer for

is inside the loop. In order to communicate the results, regrouping is called for just as it is in addition.

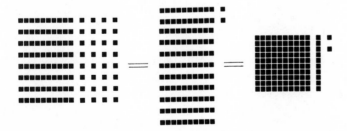

Therefore,

It is important that symbolic representation (i.e., 8 × 14 = 112) not be used at this time.

Activity 3-C2.
(representational)

•*Materials*   Paper, pencils, Work Sheet 3-C2.

•***Procedure***   Ask the students to solve the following problem by the same technique as introduced in Activity 3-C1, this time using representational notation.

Problem:

$$\vdots \times \text{——} \cdots = \text{?}$$

8 × 14 = ?

First set up the multiplication problem in array format. Students then fill in the indicated number of strips and tiles.

Step 1:

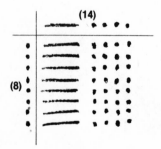

Step 2 involves regrouping the answer found in Step 1 into a more efficient form. Students should be told to regroup whenever possible. In this case there are 30 single tiles which can be traded for 3 strips. When combined with the original 8 strips and regrouped to form 1 raft (100) and 1 strip (10), the final answer can be recorded symbolically.

Step 2:

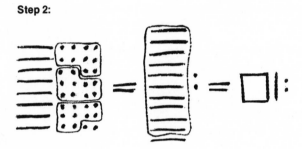

Therefore,

X — •••• = ☐ | :

8 × 14 = 112

Note: It is important that students are asked to fill-in single tiles first, then strips, then rafts as necessary. The rational for this procedure will become apparent when students are required to develop the standard symbolic algorithm for multiplication.

Have students make up similar problems for each other and record their results using symbolic notations, as above.

Name_____

Use squares, lines, and dots to solve these problems.

Example:

$$\times \begin{array}{|ccc} \overline{\quad} & \cdots \\ \vdots & \vdots \\ \vdots & \vdots \\ \vdots & \vdots \end{array} = ||||||||+\begin{array}{c}\vdots\vdots\\\vdots\vdots\\\vdots\vdots\end{array} = ||||||||+|||+\vdots = \square + | + \vdots$$

1. $\times$ —— • • •
   =   =   =

2. $\times$ —— • • • • •
   =   =   =

3. $\times$ —— • • • • • •
   =   =   =

4. $\times$ —— • • • • • • • • •
   =   =   =

5. $\times$ —— —— •
   =   =   =

•*Materials*   Pencils, paper, Work Sheet 3-C3.

•***Procedure***   In order to develop a symbolic algorithm for multiplication present the following problem in representational format:

8 × 16 =

Solve this problem with your students step by step while concurrently presenting the appropriate step of the symbolic algorithm.

Step 1   The set up

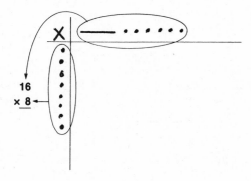

This problem is read "eight times sixteen" just as we referred to the concrete situation as "eight rows of sixteen."

Step 2   Filling In

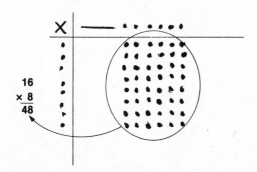

Students are asked to fill in all single tiles first. This number can then be recorded symbolically. If students have difficulty determining that a 6 × 8 array equals 48 tiles, circling groups of ten may help. The strips can then be filled in and the number of tiles recorded.

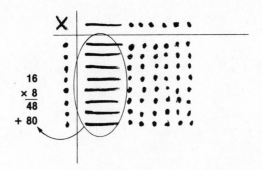

Step 3 Solution

Adding partial products provides the final solution.

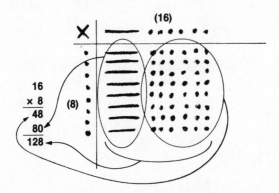

Name

Solve these problems.

Example:

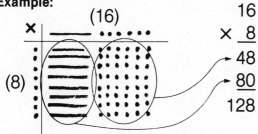

$$\begin{array}{r} 16 \\ \times \underline{8} \\ 48 \\ \underline{80} \\ 128 \end{array}$$

1. (19)
$$\begin{array}{r} 19 \\ \times \underline{6} \\ \hline \end{array}$$

(6)

5. (16)
$$\begin{array}{r} 16 \\ \times \underline{4} \\ \hline \end{array}$$

(4)

2. (13)
$$\begin{array}{r} 13 \\ \times \underline{9} \\ \hline \end{array}$$

(9)

6. (12)
$$\begin{array}{r} 12 \\ \times \underline{8} \\ \hline \end{array}$$

(8)

3. (17)
$$\begin{array}{r} 17 \\ \times \underline{5} \\ \hline \end{array}$$

(5)

7.
$$\begin{array}{r} 13 \\ \times \underline{7} \\ \hline \end{array}$$

8.
$$\begin{array}{r} 19 \\ \times \underline{9} \\ \hline \end{array}$$

4. (15)
$$\begin{array}{r} 15 \\ \times \underline{7} \\ \hline \end{array}$$

(7)

9.
$$\begin{array}{r} 16 \\ \times \underline{8} \\ \hline \end{array}$$

10.
$$\begin{array}{r} 12 \\ \times \underline{6} \\ \hline \end{array}$$

Concept D: Multiplication of a Two-Digit
by a Two-Digit Number

Activity 3-D1.
(concrete)

•*Materials*   Single tiles, tile strips, rafts, yarn.

•*Procedure*   Have students solve the following problem with tile materials:

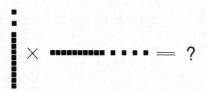

Using yarn as an array organizer on a table or floor, set up the problem as follows:

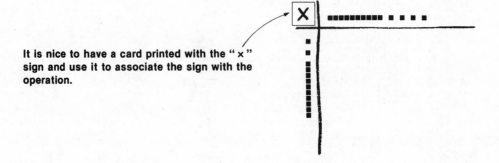

It is nice to have a card printed with the " × " sign and use it to associate the sign with the operation.

The next step is to fill in the array with units, strips, and rafts, starting with the smallest pieces first as in 3-C2.

Students fill in unit tiles as shown.

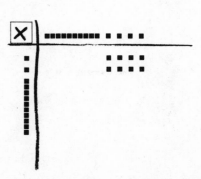

Next, students fill in wherever units and strips intersect:

Students should note that strips can be used in these instances because they are more convenient than sets of ten individual units.

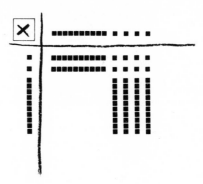

Finally, students find that the remaining space can be filled in by a raft.

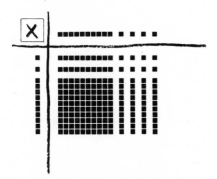

Note that this procedure produces the appropriate number of equivalent rows as required by array multiplication. Therefore, since no regrouping is necessary:

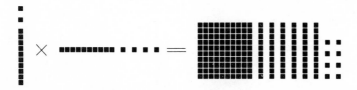

Again, it is important that students not be required to use symbolic notation at this level.

Activity 3-D2.
(representational)

•*Materials*   Paper, pencils, Work Sheet 3-D2.

•***Procedure***   Have students use representational notation to solve the following problem. Ask them to record the factors and products by means of symbolic notation as well.

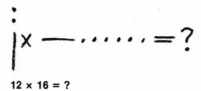

12 × 16 = ?

Using the same procedure as outlined in Activity 3-D1, students set up the problem as below.

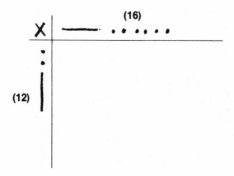

After filling in the array, step by step they will have

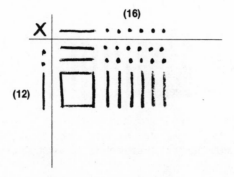

Regrouping results

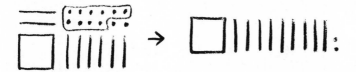

Therefore,

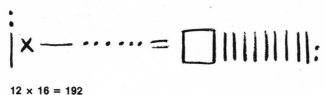

12 × 16 = 192

After completing Work Sheet 3-2D, students should make up several of these problems for each other, recording their results in symbolic notation, as above.

•*Materials*   Paper, pencils, Work Sheet 3-D3.

Activity 3-D3
(symbolic)

•***Procedure***   After considerable success with prior activities, it is appropriate to effect a transition from representational notation to use of the symbolic multiplication algorithm. Solve the following problem with students, concurrently presenting the appropriate phase of the symbolic algorithm.

Name_____

Solve these problems.

Example:

1. X| —— • • •
   _____

   = •
   =
   =
   _____

2. X| —— • • • • • •
   _____

   =
   =
   =
   _____

3. X| —— • • • • • •
   _____

   =
   =
   =
   _____

4. X| —— • • • • •
   _____

   =
   =
   =
   _____

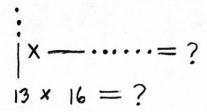

$$13 \times 16 = ?$$

Algorithm A

Step 1 The set up

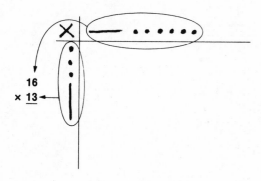

Step 2 Filling in
Using the same procedure as in the concrete phase of this activity (3-D1), students fill in the array starting with units and moving to rafts. In this phase students should record *each* partial product *as* they fill it in.

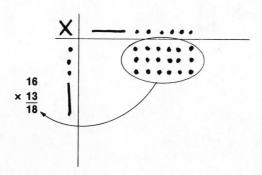

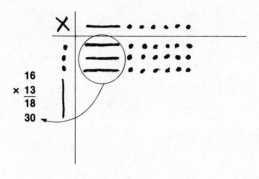

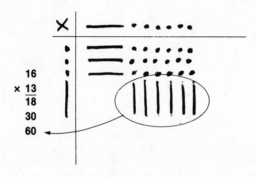

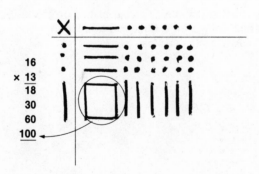

Step 3 Solution
Adding the partial products gives the final answer

```
      16
×     13
      18
      30
      60
+    100
     208
```

Combining the first two and last two partial products as below gives the standard multiplication algorithm.

Algorithm B

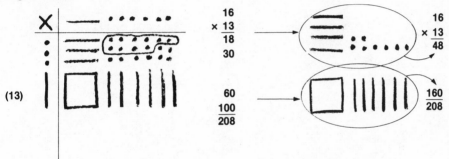

Note that Algorithms A and B are indeed equivalent. Neither is faster; neither involves less work. Algorithm A evolves directly from the representational framework and should prove quite satisfactory to most students. Algorithm B can be introduced as "a common method," but we feel that it is not essential that students move from A to B. They will choose the algorithm that works best for them. The correlation between the array method of multiplication and each multiplication algorithm should not go unnoted.

After experience with Work Sheet 3-D3, students should no longer need to rely on a pictorial representation of each problem. To facilitate this transition some students may need a direct explanation of the algorithm strictly at the symbolic level. For example:

```
     45
×    23
```

A.   Beginning with the units-place multiplier, we multiply 3 × 5

```
     45
×    23
     15
```

B. Next, we move to the unit multiplier times the tens-place multiplicand
3 × 40

```
    45
×   23
    15
   120
```

C. Since we have completed multiplying by the units place, we multiply
the one's place (5) multiplicand by the ten's place multiplier 20 × 5

```
    45
×   23
    15
   120
   100
```

D. Finally, we multiply the ten's place multiplicand by the ten's place
multiplier 20 × 40

```
    45
×   23
    15
   120
   100
   800
```

E. We then add all the partial products to find the answer:

```
    45
×   23
    15
   120
   100
+  800
  1035 Voila!
```

Name_____

Solve the following problems.

Example:

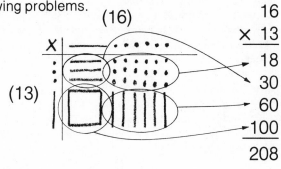

$$
\begin{array}{r}
16 \\
\times\ 13 \\
\hline
18 \\
30 \\
60 \\
100 \\
\hline
208
\end{array}
$$

1. (12) (14)

$$
\begin{array}{r}
12 \\
\times\ 14 \\
\end{array}
$$

4. (16) (19)

$$
\begin{array}{r}
16 \\
\times\ 19 \\
\end{array}
$$

2. (15) (15)

$$
\begin{array}{r}
15 \\
\times\ 15 \\
\end{array}
$$

5. (17) (12)

$$
\begin{array}{r}
17 \\
\times\ 12 \\
\end{array}
$$

3. (18) (17)

6.

$$
\begin{array}{r}
18 \\
\times\ 17 \\
\end{array}
\qquad
\begin{array}{r}
13 \\
\times\ 19 \\
\end{array}
\qquad
\begin{array}{r}
15 \\
\times\ 12 \\
\end{array}
\qquad
\begin{array}{r}
14 \\
\times\ 17 \\
\end{array}
\qquad
\begin{array}{r}
13 \\
\times\ 26 \\
\end{array}
$$

Division

Division is an elementary mathematical concept with which a substantial number of students have difficulty. As traditionally presented, the division algorithm makes little more sense to children than does magic. Students find themselves blindly following a formula to achieve the "right" answer to an irrelevant question. We feel that our approach to the teaching of division epitomizes the value of a developmental approach to elementary mathematics.

The procedures in this section parallel those in the multiplication section. They start with repeated subtraction, which provides a meaningful physical definition for the division operation. As this approach becomes unwieldy, we turn to a partitioning-and-array model that is analogous to the array model for multiplication. Let's try 132 ÷ 11.

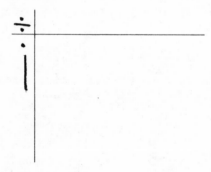

First make eleven equal rows with the biggest pieces possible.

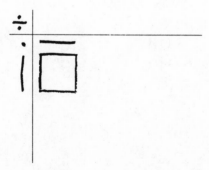

With left over, continue adding to each row using the largest pieces possible and taking care to keep all the rows even.

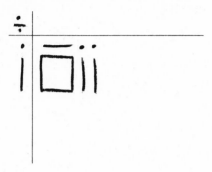

Finally, reproduce the top row above the array. This represents the answer.

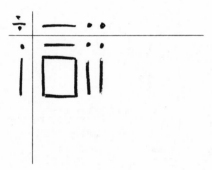

Note how the division algorithm is derived from this representational model.

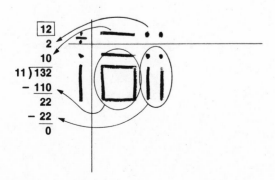

Students are able to improve their estimates as they gain experience with this approach. The following, for example, is not a "wrong" answer, even though there is a shorter way to do it. Such "mistakes" will lead students to a firmer understanding of the nature of division.

$$
\begin{array}{r}
\boxed{12} \\
1 \\
1 \\
10 \\
11\,\overline{)132} \\
-110 \\
\hline
22 \\
-11 \\
\hline
11 \\
-11 \\
\hline
0
\end{array}
$$

As was the case with the first multiplication algorithm, we feel that this division algorithm is more closely linked with the physical world than is the standard algorithm. As students gain familiarity with this algorithm and become better estimators, they will discover on their own the traditional shortcut.

$$
\begin{array}{r}
1 \\
11\,\overline{)132} \\
-110 \\
\end{array}
\quad\Rightarrow\quad
\begin{array}{r}
12 \\
11\,\overline{)132} \\
-110 \\
\hline
22 \\
-22 \\
\hline
0
\end{array}
$$

Division may become less "magic" after these experiences have enabled children to develop more thorough comprehension of this difficult concept. (See Appendix 1 for discussion of readiness diagnosis for division.)

Concept A: Division as Repeated Subtraction

Activity 4-A1.
(concrete)

• *Materials*   A quantity of wooden cubes.

• *Procedure*   Ask students to line up twelve blocks;

then have them remove three blocks at a time

and stack them

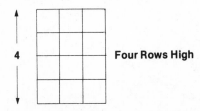

Four Rows High

and record the number of rows in the stacks.
Record the procedure (12 ÷ 3 = 4) and continue with additional problems,
with and without remainders.

•*Materials*   Work Sheet 4-A2, with different numbers of objects, similar
to the following:

Activity 4-A2.
(representational)

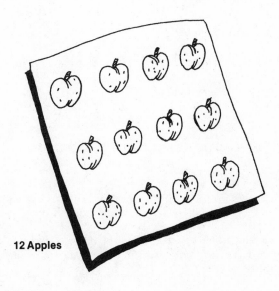

12 Apples

•**Procedure**   Have students draw a bag around each set of three apples, keeping track of the number of bags.

4 Bags

Record as follows: 12 ÷ 3 = 4.

Activity 4-A3.
(symbolic)

•*Materials*   Paper, pencils, work Sheet 4-A3.

•**Procedure**   Use the following division algorithm to solve the problem:

```
      4
  3 ) 12
    − 3   1
      9
    − 3   1
      6
    − 3   1
      3
    − 3  +1
      0   4
```

It is important to distinguish between two types of division commonly taught at the elementary level. For example, there are two ways to arrange beans in order to demonstrate 6 ÷ 3 = 2.

Name_____

How many bags do you need?

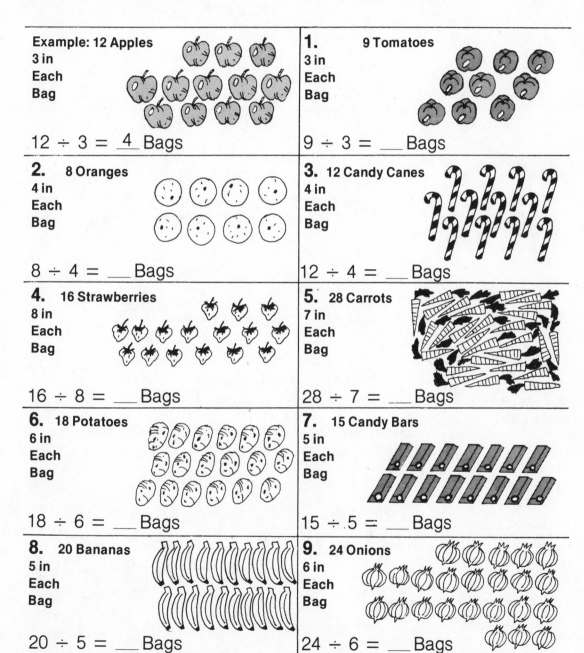

Example: 12 Apples
3 in
Each
Bag

$12 \div 3 =$ _4_ Bags

1. 9 Tomatoes
3 in
Each
Bag

$9 \div 3 =$ ___ Bags

2. 8 Oranges
4 in
Each
Bag

$8 \div 4 =$ ___ Bags

3. 12 Candy Canes
4 in
Each
Bag

$12 \div 4 =$ ___ Bags

4. 16 Strawberries
8 in
Each
Bag

$16 \div 8 =$ ___ Bags

5. 28 Carrots
7 in
Each
Bag

$28 \div 7 =$ ___ Bags

6. 18 Potatoes
6 in
Each
Bag

$18 \div 6 =$ ___ Bags

7. 15 Candy Bars
5 in
Each
Bag

$15 \div 5 =$ ___ Bags

8. 20 Bananas
5 in
Each
Bag

$20 \div 5 =$ ___ Bags

9. 24 Onions
6 in
Each
Bag

$24 \div 6 =$ ___ Bags

Repeated Subtraction:

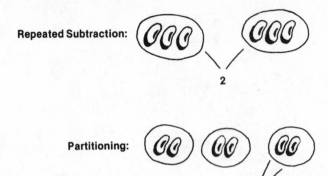

Partitioning:

The former method demonstrates how many threes in six. The latter demonstrates how many beans in each of three equal groups. Both are symbolized like this:

6 ÷ 3 = 2

Since repeated subtraction logically follows from the repeated-addition definition of multiplication, we prefer its use as an introduction to division. Later, it becomes important that students be able to recognize both situations when they arise and to apply the division algorithm uniformly.

Concept B: Division Using Arrays

Activity 4-B1.
(concrete)

•*Materials*   A quantity of ceramic tiles.

•*Procedure*   The task is to divide a group of tiles evenly among six friends.

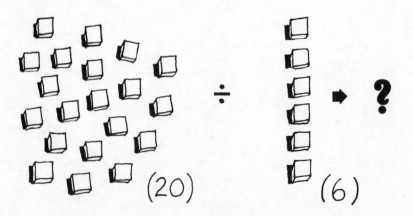

Name_____

Solve these division problems.

Example:

$$
\begin{array}{r}
4 \\
3\overline{)12} \\
-3 \quad 1 \\
\hline
9 \\
-3 \quad 1 \\
\hline
6 \\
-3 \quad 1 \\
\hline
3 \\
-3 \quad +1 \\
\hline
0 \quad 4
\end{array}
\qquad
\begin{array}{r}
2 \\
4\overline{)8} \\
-4 \quad 1 \\
\hline
4 \\
-4 \quad +1 \\
\hline
0 \quad 2
\end{array}
$$

1. $2\overline{)8}$

2. $3\overline{)9}$

3. $5\overline{)20}$

4. $6\overline{)18}$

5. $4\overline{)16}$

6. $7\overline{)42}$

7. $9\overline{)27}$

8. $8\overline{)32}$

9. $6\overline{)30}$

On the graph below, put six tiles in the friends column to represent the six friends. Next, place one tile at a time in the columns beside each friend until all the tiles are gone. The only rule is that all the rows must be exactly the same length (the friends must each have the same number of tiles). Any leftovers go into the box at the top right.

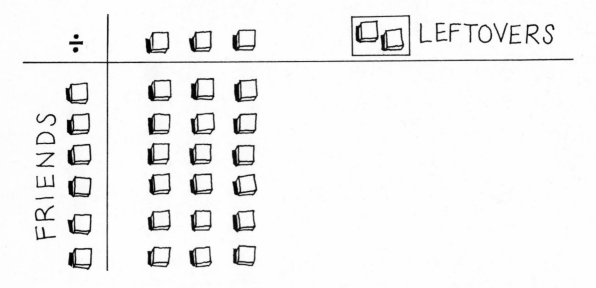

It should be pointed out that not only are the tiles being divided among six friends, but that six additional tiles are used to *represent* the friends. In the sort of division problems that students will be likely to encounter during their daily lives, the divisor generally represents something quite different from the dividend. Activities like 4-B2 provide experiences in which numerals represent various concrete situations and are not simply symbols of abstract ideas.

Activity 4-B2
(representational)

• *Materials*   Paper, pencils, Work Sheet 4-B2.

• *Procedure*   To provide a real world model of division using the array method, propose the following problem to your students: "If you want to build a raft and you have six poles and twenty nails, what is the greatest number of cross beams that can be used to fasten the poles together?" (You must use one nail every time a pole and cross member meet.)

Students should first make a concrete or graphic representation of the problem, understanding that each cross beam requires six nails.

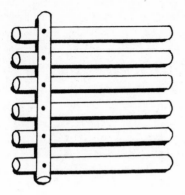

Cross beams should then be "nailed" in place one at a time until there is no longer a sufficient number of nails to secure another one.

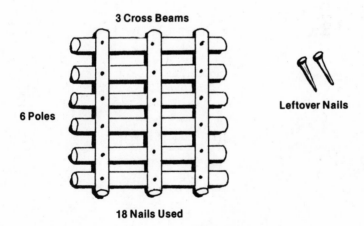

3 Cross Beams

6 Poles

Leftover Nails

18 Nails Used

Students should realize that two nails are left over. The problem can now be recorded as

20 + 6 = 3 with 2 left over

After working through this problem with your students, Work Sheet 4-B2 can be utilized.

Name_____

Solve these division problems:

Example:

How many cross beams can go on a raft with 6 poles if you only have 20 nails?

$20 \div 6 = 3$ with 2 left over

1. 8 poles and 35 nails?

$35 \div 5 = \underline{}$ with $\underline{}$ left over

2. 5 poles and 28 nails?

$28 \div 5 = \underline{}$ with $\underline{}$ left over

3. 7 poles and 16 nails?

$16 \div 7 = \underline{}$ with $\underline{}$ left over

4. 9 poles and 36 nails?

$36 \div 9 = \underline{}$ with $\underline{}$ left over

5. 4 poles with 27 nails?

$27 \div 4 = \underline{}$ with $\underline{}$ left over

• *Materials*   Paper, pencils, work Sheet 4-B3.

• ***Procedure***   Give students a problem such as the following: "If you want to build a raft with eight poles and you have thirty-five nails, what is the greatest number of cross beams you can use?"

```
         4  remainder 3
    8 ) 35
       − 8 | 1
        27
       − 8 | 1
        19
       − 8 | 1
        11
       − 8 | +1
         3 | 4
```

Remember this number represents the amount of nails

8) 35 ◂

and this one the number of poles.

Concept C: Division

• *Materials*   Tiles, tile strips.

• ***Procedure***   Ask students to solve the following problem using tile strips and the array method.

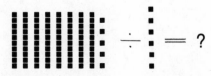

85 ÷ 6 = ?

(Numbers are for teacher reference only.)

Name_____

How many crossbeams can you put on these rafts?

Example: 8 poles and 35 nails

$$
\begin{array}{r}
4 \quad \text{with 3 left over} \\
8\overline{)35} \\
-8 \quad | \quad 1 \\
\overline{27} \\
-8 \quad | \quad 1 \\
\overline{19} \\
-8 \quad | \quad 1 \\
\overline{11} \\
-8 \quad | +1 \\
\overline{3} \quad | \quad 4
\end{array}
$$

1. $6\overline{)35}$

2. $4\overline{)21}$

3. $9\overline{)39}$

4. $6\overline{)23}$

5. $7\overline{)49}$

6. $3\overline{)23}$

7. $5\overline{)25}$

8. $8\overline{)43}$

First, have them place one tile strip in each row.

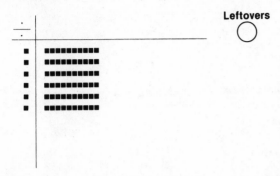

If they had enough strips, they would make an additional column. Since there are not enough, students must break up what is left of the strips (i.e., tens), combine these loose tiles with original six (ones), and distribute them uniformly throughout the rows. The answer is the top row reproduced above the array (similar to the arrangement for multiplication).

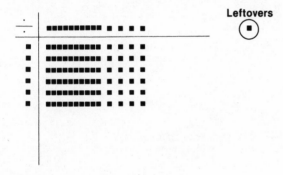

Therefore,

Go through several examples using only concrete materials. Do not attempt to correlate the activity with symbolic notation at this time.

Activity 4-C2.
(representational)

• *Materials*   Paper, pencils, Work Sheet 4-C2.

• ***Procedure***   Have students solve problems using our representational notation.

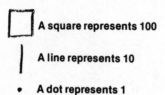

A square represents 100

A line represents 10

A dot represents 1

Pose a problem, using symbolic notation along with representational notation.

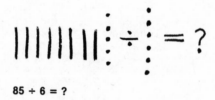

85 ÷ 6 = ?

Ask students to follow the same sequence of solution.

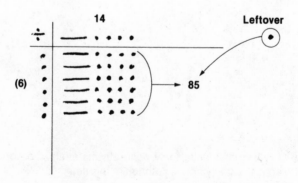

Therefore,

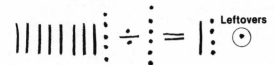

85 ÷ 6 = 14 remainder 1

•*Materials*   Paper, pencils, Work Sheet 4-C3.

•***Procedure***   To help students begin to use the division algorithm, propose the following problem:

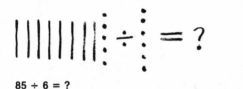

85 ÷ 6 = ?

Step 1   As students set up the problem on the organizer, introduce the symbolic record explaining the relationship between the picture and the symbols.

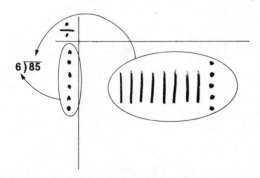

Step 2   The tiles are evenly divided among the six rows, using the largest pieces first. A symbolic record is then made, indicating that 60 tiles are in place; 10 in each row.

Name_____

Use tile strips to solve these problems. Remember, keep all rows
the same length.

Example:

14   left over

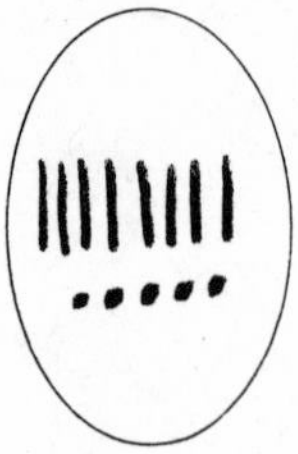

$$85 \div 6 = 14 \quad 1$$

remainder

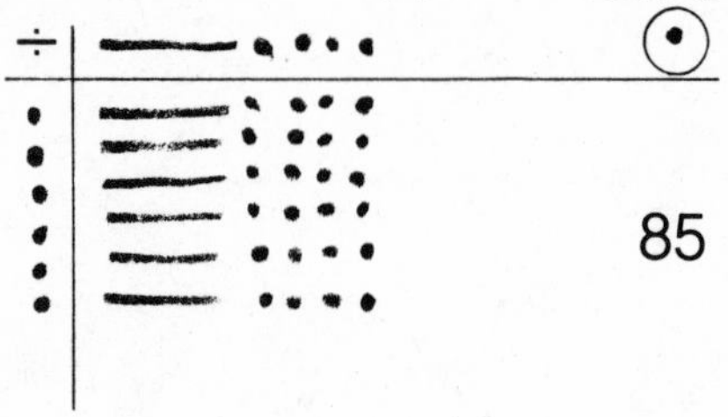

85

1.

$$73 \div 7 = \underline{\quad} r.\underline{\quad}$$

7   73

2.

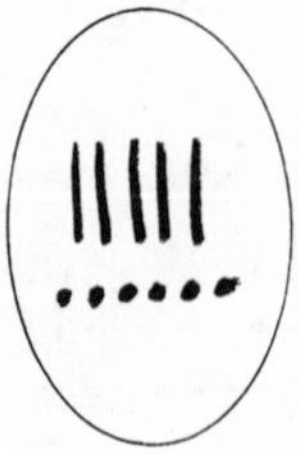

$$56 \div 5 = \underline{\quad} r.\underline{\quad}$$

5   56

3.

$$83 \div 4 = \underline{\quad} r.\underline{\quad}$$

4   83

4.

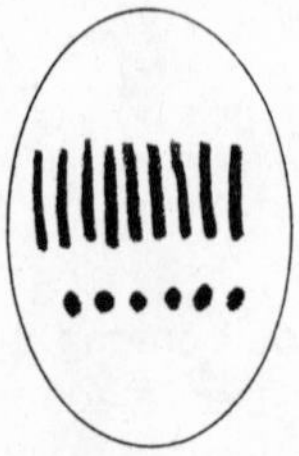

$$96 \div 8 = \underline{\quad} r.\underline{\quad}$$

8   96

From *Mathmatters*, copyright © 1978 by Goodyear Publishing Company, Inc.

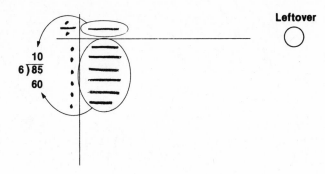

Leftover

Step 3 In order to keep the rows even, the two leftover strips need to be traded for individual tiles. When these plus the original five tiles are combined, 25 tiles are left to distribute. Point out the symbolic method for determining the amount remaining (that is, $85 - 60 = 25$).

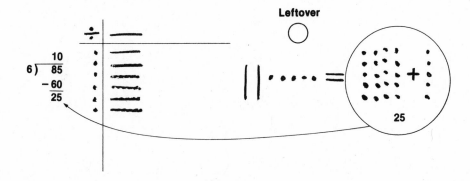

Step 4 The remaining tiles can now be divided evenly and recorded as in Step 2. The number of remaining tiles are placed in the "leftover" box.

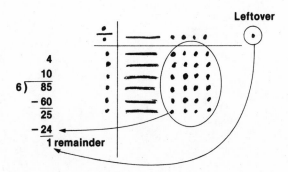

Name_____

Solve these problems. Use dots and lines if you need help.

Example:

```
 14  r. 1           1    4    remainder 1
  4
 10
6) 85
-60
 25
-24
  1
```

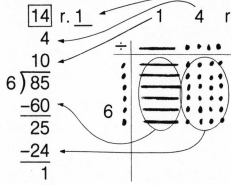

85

1. 4) 67   ÷ |_____

2. 6) 96   ÷ |_____

3. 5) 78   ÷ |_____

4. 7) 92   ÷ |_____

5. 4) 91   ÷ |_____

6. 3) 48   ÷ |_____

Students now add upwards to determine the final answer, recording symbolically as follows:

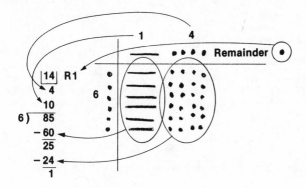

Concept D: Division of a Three-Digit Number by a One-Digit Number

•*Materials*   Single tiles, tile strips, rafts.

Activity 4-D1.
(concrete)

Note   Materials such as bean sticks, Dienes blocks, Number Blox, or Cuisenaire blocks, squares, and rods can be used in place of tile strips (see Appendix III).

•*Procedure*   Ask students to solve the following problem using tile strips and the array method.

145   ÷ 5 = ?   **(Numbers are for teacher reference only.)**

They should follow the same procedure as before, distributing the rafts and strips first. (Note that in this case the raft must be exchanged for ten tile strips.)

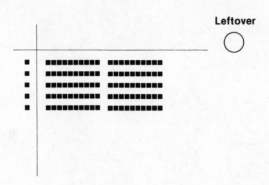

The remaining tens are then exchanged for ones and the array is completed.

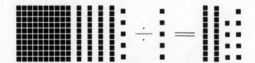

Therefore,

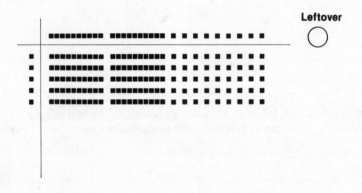

•*Materials*   Paper, pencils, Work Sheet 4-D2.

•**Procedure**   Ask students to solve the following problem using representational notation. At this point, they should also use symbolic notation along with representational notation.

□ ||||⦂ ÷ ⦂ = ?

145 ÷ 5 = ?

The same procedures as introduced previously are used in solving the problem.

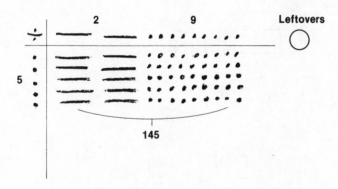

Therefore,

□ ||||⦂ ÷ ⦂ = ||⦂

145 ÷ 5 = 29

Name_____

Use squares, lines, and dots to help solve these problems.

Example:

145 ◻||||⋮ $145 \div 5 =$ _____$^{r.}$_____

1.

7

163 ◻||||||⋮ $163 \div 7 =$ _____$^{r.}$_____

2.

9

275 ◻◻||||||⋮ $275 \div 9 =$ _____$^{r.}$_____

3.

8

137 ◻|||⋮ $137 \div 8 =$ _____$^{r.}$_____

4.

6

115 ◻|⋮ $115 \div 6 =$ _____$^{r.}$_____

•*Materials*   Paper, pencils, Work Sheet 4-D3.

•***Procedure***   Develop the division algorithm for 3-place dividends by proposing the following problem:

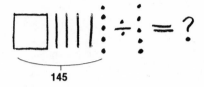

145

Go through the step by step process as in Activity 4-C3, recording as indicated.

Step 1   Set up problem and record.

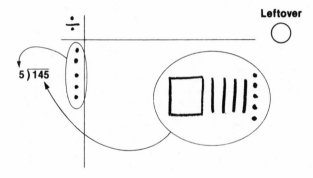

Step 2   The raft must be exchanged for strips first, since there are not enough rafts to put one in each row. These, when combined with the original 4 strips can be evenly divided among the 6 rows and recorded

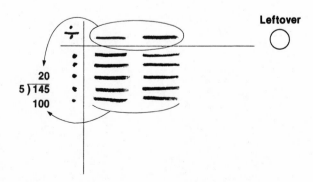

Step 3   Since only four strips are left over, they must be traded for individual tiles. When these plus the original five tiles are combined, we have 45 tiles left. This amount can then be recorded symbolically as below

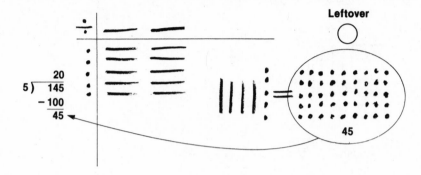

Step 4   The remaining division can now be completed and recorded as in Step 2.

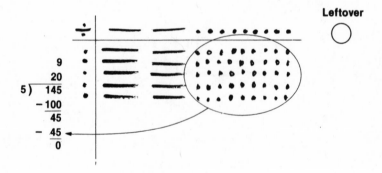

Students now add upwards to determine their final answer.

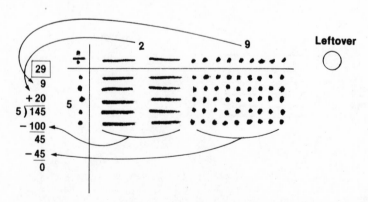

Name_____

Solve these problems.

Example:

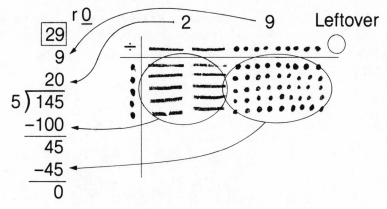

r 0

29

9

20

5)‾1‾4‾5‾

−100

45

−45

0

1. 9)‾1‾3‾8‾ ÷ _____

2. 8)‾2‾5‾9‾ ÷ _____

3. 7)‾3‾7‾4‾ ÷ _____

4. 5)‾1‾8‾9‾ ÷ _____

5. 6)‾2‾8‾3‾ ÷ _____

6. 8)‾1‾2‾5‾ ÷ _____

Concept E: Division of a Three-Digit number by a Two-Digit Number

Activity 4-E1.
(concrete)

•*Materials*   Single tiles, tile strips, rafts.

•***Procedure***   Ask students to solve the following problem using tile strips and the array method.

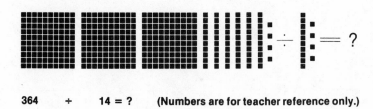

364   ÷   14 = ?   **(Numbers are for teacher reference only.)**

Have them follow the same techniques as for solving the previous division problems. When the divisor is arranged on the left side of the array, the loose tiles should be placed above the tile strip. Tell students to fill in the array with the dividend, using the biggest pieces first. There must be the same number of tiles in each column as there are in the divisor.

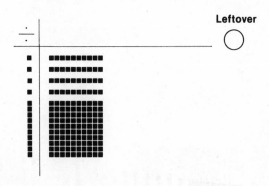

Leftover

Note that the above arrangement is the simplest possible under the circumstances. Students must continue filling in the array until there aren't enough tile strips left to complete a column. A raft must be broken in order to complete the next column.

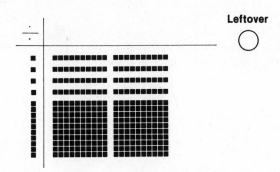

There are now eight tile strips and four loose tiles left to be distributed. Laying down one tile strip at a time and trading for loose tiles whenever necessary facilitates completion of the distribution.

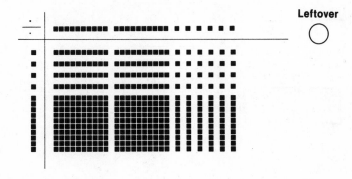

Therefore,

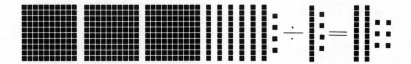

Give several problems of this type without requiring symbolic notation. Make sure that some will have remainders.

Activity 4-E2.
(representational)

• *Materials*   Paper, pencils, Work Sheet 4-E2.

• ***Procedure***   Have children solve the following problem using representational notation. Ask them to use symbolic notation as well.

The same procedures as previously introduced should be used to solve the problem.

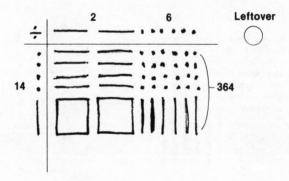

Therefore,

364   ÷   14   =   26

Name_____

Use tile strips to solve these problems.

Example:

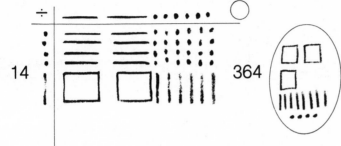

2   6   Leftover

14   364

$364 \div 14 = \underline{26}^{r.}\underline{0}$

1.

18   297

$297 \div 18 = \underline{}^{r.}\underline{}$

2.

12   324

$324 \div 12 = \underline{}^{r.}\underline{}$

3.

16   527

$527 \div 16 = \underline{}^{r.}\underline{}$

Activity 4-E3.
(symbolic)

•*Materials*   Paper, pencils, Work Sheet 4-E3.

•**Procedure**   In order to develop the division algorithm for multi-digit divisors, propose the following problem to your students.

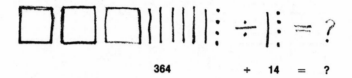

364   ÷   14   =   ?

Step 1   Have each student set up the problem on the organizer and record it symbolically as below.

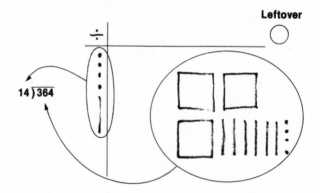

Step 2   Evenly divide the bag of tiles by using the biggest pieces first, taking care to keep the rows even.

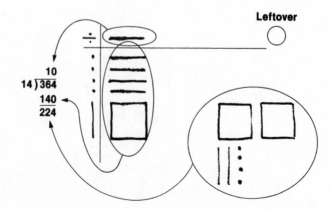

It becomes evident that it is more efficient to leave the raft intact than to trade for 10 strips, remembering that each tile in the multiplier still corresponds to 1 strip. Point out the relationship indicated by the arrows above and between the pictorial representation and the symbolic record.

Step 3 Since there are not sufficient tile strips remaining to distribute 10 tiles to each row, it is necessary to exchange one of the remaining rafts for 10 tile strips.

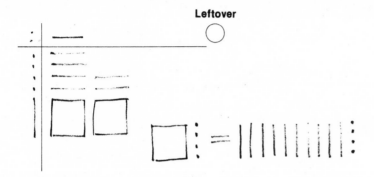

The result should appear as below:

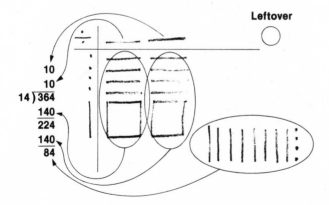

Note: As students gain experience using tile materials and the array division method, they will begin to visualize solutions before completing the required trades. In the above instance students may realize that there are enough tiles for each row to have 2 strips for 20 tiles before actually trading in the left over raft.

```
                                          10
           20                             10
       14)364                         14)364
          280        instead of          140
           84                            224
                                         140
                                          84
```

Students will discover many meaningful shortcuts of this type as they gain experience with this division method.

Since 84 tiles are left, the students should continue dividing the bag of tiles. In order to keep all the rows equal it is necessary to exchange 2 tile strips for 20 unit tiles.

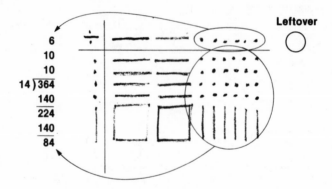

Leftover

```
       6
      10
      10
  14)364
     140
     224
     140
      84
```

Name_____

Solve these problems.

Example:

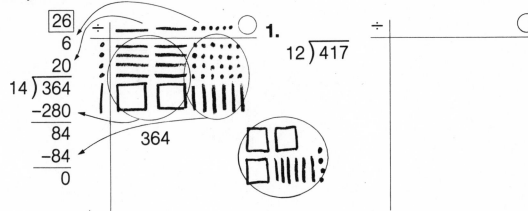

$$\boxed{26} \div$$

$$\begin{array}{r} 6 \\ 20 \\ 14\overline{)364} \\ -280 \\ \hline 84 \\ -84 \\ \hline 0 \end{array}$$

364

1. $12\overline{)417}$ $\div$ ◯

$\div$ ◯

2. $15\overline{)326}$ $\div$ ◯

3. $16\overline{)512}$ $\div$ ◯

4. $18\overline{)271}$ $\div$ ◯

5. $23\overline{)690}$ $\div$ ◯

Step 4   Students now add upwards and record their answer.

Note the similarity between the array method of division and the algorithm. Once students become familiar and comfortable with this algorithm, they will begin to discover and employ their own shortcuts.

They may notice that the first algorithm always gives them a "place-holder" zero in the ones column. This discovery can be reinforced by class discussion, but we feel that it does not call for a separate work sheet.

Notes for Topic 4

Fraction Operations*

Children develop an early familiarity with fractions through day-to-day family interactions. Sharing is one common activity that requires knowledge of fractional parts. If two children share a piece of cake, a good way to ensure tranquility is to have one child divide the cake into two pieces and let the other child choose first! The partitioning of objects and groups is fundamental to the fraction concept. Schoolchildren have already had many experiences that can be developed into a sound understanding of elementary fractions.

Two conceptual models are commonly used in order to build an understanding of fractional relationships. The first model can be demonstrated by giving three children thirty marbles and asking them to partition the set into three groups so that each has an equal number of marbles. Once all three are satisfied with the result, each group can safely be called a third. Children learn the language of fractions (i.e., *one third*) before acquiring a formal understanding of the ratio concept of fraction (i.e., $\frac{1}{3}$.)

The use of the set model presupposes a thorough understanding of conservation of number. A child who is a nonconserver of number may perceive the whole set as being somehow different than the sum of its parts and therefore may not develop a proper understanding of fractional partitioning. Avoid using this model until such understanding develops.

The second model is based on parts of a whole rather than on parts of a set. This model generally utilizes the attribute of area (e.g., parts of a pie), although volume (liters) and mass (grams and kilograms) are sometimes used as well. When fractional parts of an area model are being defined, it is necessary that each child thoroughly understand conservation of area. Appendix I provides activities to help the teacher evaluate this readiness.

An area model utilizing parts of a whole is not only an effective means of defining fractional parts, it also very efficiently extends this concept to the performance of operations with fractions. Children should be encouraged to utilize concrete models representing complicated rational operations until adequate conceptual understanding has been developed. Symbolic manipulation should take on deeper meaning as a result. The materials used in this section (fraction tiles, geoboards, etc.) are examples of such concrete models.

---

*''Seeing Through Fractions'' Portions of this introduction have been reprinted by special permission of *Learning, The Magazine for Creative Teaching,* March 1977. © 1977 by Education Today Company, Inc., 530 University Ave., Palo Alto, CA 94301.

Before we proceed with the instructional activities in this section, one final comment seems appropriate. Though common fractions will remain a part of our everyday language, computation with fractions may soon go the way of the steam engine and the windup watch. With the advent of the metric system of measurement in the United States and the increased usage of inexpensive hand-held calculators, even the infamous "junior-high fractions" (e.g., $\frac{7}{32}$, $\frac{17}{51}$, $\frac{123}{769}$, etc.) will give way to simpler decimal notation for keeping track of the numbers between zero and one. Several states are already testing curricula designed to teach decimal concepts in the middle grades and to place less emphasis on common fractions. In the meantime, however, it is important to provide students with experiences that will aid their development of a sound understanding of fractional relationships.

Concept A: Fractional Parts of a Set (Partitioning)

Activity 5-A1.
(concrete)

•*Materials*   Loose tiles or other counters.

•***Procedure***   Give each pair of students an even-numbered pile of counters. The first student divides the pile in half, and the second student chooses the half he or she wants. If both students are satisfied with their piles, they have defined one-half.

To define other simple fractions, have students work in larger groups. In a group of four students, the first student divides the stack into four piles. The next two students readjust the piles as evenly as possible. Student number four picks first, then students one, two, and three. If all four are satisfied with the size of their piles, then they have defined one fourth.

The names of the various partitions are used (i.e., one half, one fourth, etc.), but no discussion of the symbolic representation ($\frac{1}{4}$) should be attempted at this time.

Activity 5-A2.
(representational)

•*Materials*   Tiles, paper, pencils.

•***Procedure***   Give each group of three or four students a stack of tiles and ask that they distribute them evenly and record their results on charts similar to the one below, drawing squares to represent tiles. Students may use the partitioning technique developed in Activity 5-A1, or they may utilize repeated subtraction by distributing the tiles one by one to each member of the group until all tiles have been handed out. Note the similarity between these techniques and the definitions of division. Ask questions: "How much of the stack did José get?" "How many did each one get?" "Did everyone get the same?" "How much of the original stack did both José and Lyn get together?"

Students

José	Lynn	Michelle
▢ ▢ ▢ ▢	▢ ▢ ▢ ▢	▢ ▢ ▢ ▢

Recording the results with fractional terms or symbols is encouraged. For example,

1. José got one third (⅓) of the stack.

2. One-third (⅓) of this stack is four tiles.

3. José and Lynn together got two-thirds (2/3) of the stack.

The students should discover the names of fractions by recording how many groups are being considered out of the total number of equal groups.

1. Consider one group out of four equal groups   one fourth ($\frac{1}{4}$)

2. Consider two groups out of three equal groups   two thirds ($\frac{2}{3}$)

3. Consider three groups out of five equal groups   three fifths ($\frac{3}{5}$)

Activity 5-A3.
(symbolic)

•*Materials*   Paper, pencils, Work Sheet 5-A3.

•*Procedure*   Students apply their notion of fractional division of groups by solving word problems developed by the teacher and other students. Encourage the students to validate their results by means of concrete materials or sketches.

Example 1. "If four people were to evenly divide a bag of twenty-four M & M's, what *fractional part* would each receive? *How many* M & M's would each receive?"

1	2	3	4
● ● ● ● ● ●	● ● ● ● ● ●	● ● ● ● ● ●	● ● ● ● ● ●
$\frac{1}{4}$	$\frac{1}{4}$	$\frac{1}{4}$	$\frac{1}{4}$
One Fourth	**One Fourth**	**One Fourth**	**One Fourth**

Example 2. "If Renee, Rosa, and Marie were to divide twelve oranges evenly, what *fractional part* would Renee and Rosa receive together? *How many* oranges would they receive?"

○ ○ ○ ○	○ ○ ○ ○	○ ○ ○ ○
$\frac{1}{3}$	$\frac{1}{3}$	$\frac{1}{3}$
One Third	**One Third**	**One Third**

Children should use fraction words (i.e., *one fourth*) before fraction symbols (i.e., $\frac{1}{4}$). Simple numbers such as one half, two thirds, one fourth, three fifths, and one tenth should form the basis for further elementary-fraction concept development. Fractions encountered in life are usually the result of some measurement activity or sharing situation and rarely require more complicated divisions. "Junior-high fractions," such as twenty-one twenty-fifths, nineteen thirty-seconds, or seventeen fifty-firsts, are generally encountered only in school. Little benefit is derived from developing operational proficiency with such numbers.

Name_____

Use the table below to help you divide eighteen apples evenly
among six children.

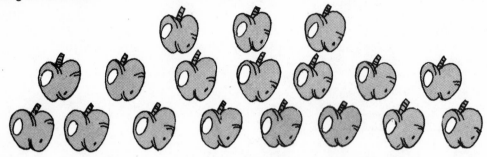

Al	José	Renee	JoAnn	Marie	Bill

How many apples would each child receive? _____

What fractional part of the bag of apples would each child

receive? _____

What fractional part would the girls receive? _____

José and Renee? _____

Concept B: Fractional Parts of a Whole

•*Materials*   Foods that can be cut into pieces.

Activity 5-B1.
(concrete)

•***Procedure***   A group of students is given an apple, a sandwich, or some other easily partitioned food and asked to divide it using the method that was used to divide the tiles in Activity 5-A1. Everyone must be satisfied with the partitioning. The last person to adjust the partitioning must make the portions as equal as possible because since he chooses last, the smallest piece will probably be left to him. If everyone ends up happy, the groups have defined the appropriate fraction.

Thirds

Sandwich

•*Materials*   Geoboards, Work Sheet 5-B2.

Activity 5-B2.
*(concrete/
representational)*

•***Procedure***   The teacher puts a rubber band of one color around the outside edge of each geoboard. Each student is asked to divide his geoboard in half with a different-colored rubber band.

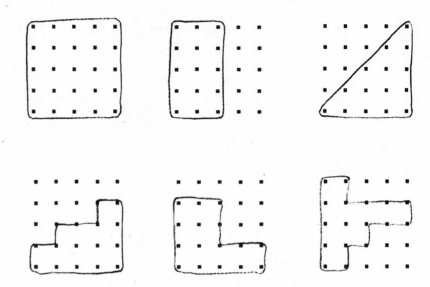

The board may be divided in half in a variety of ways. Students should be asked to find as many different ways as they can. Encourage them to define some criterion for "halfness" that all of these representations have in common (i.e., the number of little squares in each partition).

This activity can be repeated with one fourth, one eighth, and even one sixteenth if desired. Rubber bands can be placed so as to define smaller fields, thus allowing introduction of other fractions.

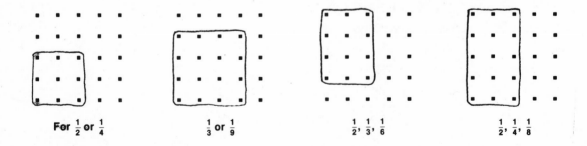

For $\frac{1}{2}$ or $\frac{1}{4}$ $\frac{1}{3}$ or $\frac{1}{9}$ $\frac{1}{2}$, $\frac{1}{3}$, $\frac{1}{6}$ $\frac{1}{2}$, $\frac{1}{4}$, $\frac{1}{8}$

Name_____

How many ways can you show one half (1/2) on the geoboards
below?

Example:

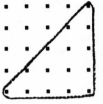

Record the following fractions.

$$\frac{1}{4} \qquad \frac{2}{4} \qquad \frac{3}{4} \qquad \frac{1}{8} \qquad \frac{2}{8}$$

$$\frac{3}{8} \qquad \frac{5}{8} \qquad \frac{1}{16} \qquad \frac{4}{16} \qquad \frac{15}{16}$$

Activity 5-B3.
(representational)

•*Materials*   Graph paper, pencils.

•***Procedure***   Graph paper is cut to various sizes to represent the areas of the geoboard fields defined in Activity 5-B2. Using only rectangles (no triangles), students fill in squares to represent the various fractions. Several versions of each fraction may be obtained. The teacher should point out that each figure in each group represents one member of a family of equivalent fractions ($\frac{1}{2}$, $\frac{2}{4}$, $\frac{4}{8}$, $\frac{6}{12}$, $\frac{8}{16}$). Reducing fractions takes on added meaning for children after such experiences.

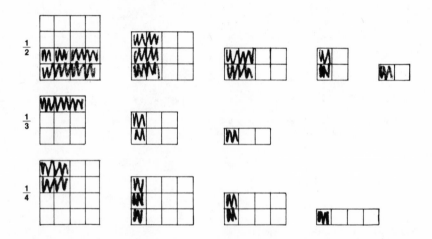

Ask the students which representation would be the "simplest" way to show one half, one third, or one fourth. In each case, the simplest representation is the last one in each row above: one out of two, one out of three, one out of four.

These pictures will be representing those fractions in subsequent activities.

•*Materials*   Graph paper, pencils, Work Sheet 5-B4.

•*Procedure*   Once students have become sufficiently familiar with the names *one half, one third,* etc., along with both concrete and pictorial representations, they should discover that there is exactly one "simplest" representation for each fraction.

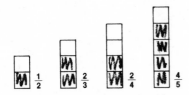

Give students fractions such as two thirds, three fifths, three tenths, etc., and have them construct the simplest pictorial representation on graph paper.

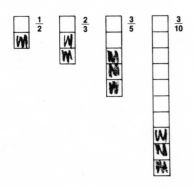

Concept C: Addition and Subtraction of Fractions with Like Denominators

•*Materials*   Colored acetate with which to construct fraction tiles.

•*Procedure*   Have each student construct a set of fraction tiles by cutting similar squares of colored acetate into equal pieces. Each square should be a different color, and each color should be cut to represent a different fraction (see Appendix III).

Name_____

Record the simplest picture of each fraction below.

		$\frac{1}{2}$			$\frac{1}{3}$			$\frac{2}{3}$				$\frac{6}{8}$			$\frac{1}{4}$		
		$\frac{2}{10}$			$\frac{3}{5}$			$\frac{3}{10}$				$\frac{10}{10}$					

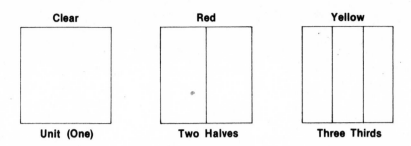

Clear

Unit (One)

Red

Two Halves

Yellow

Three Thirds

Ask students to choose two tiles of the same color and put them together (in this case the student has chosen two fourths).

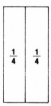

$\frac{1}{4}$ $\frac{1}{4}$

Placing them on the unit tile (a tile that was not cut into fractions) we see that they cover one half the area.

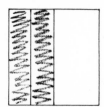

Placing them on the one-half tile, we see that they match.

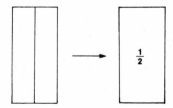

$\frac{1}{2}$

Have students work in pairs to make up their own problems.

At this point, tiles should be called by their word names (*one half, one fourth,* etc.). The use of symbolic notation is not encouraged at this level.

Activity 5-C2.
*(concrete/
representational)*

•*Materials*   Fraction tiles.

•***Procedure***   The students should try to discover as many ways as possible of combining like fractional parts to make one. They should record their activities by sketching.

$$\frac{1}{3} \quad + \quad \frac{2}{3} \quad = \quad 1 \qquad\qquad \frac{2}{3} \quad + \quad \frac{1}{3} \quad = \quad 1$$

$$\frac{1}{3} \quad + \quad \frac{1}{3} \quad + \quad \frac{1}{3} \quad = \quad 1$$

Graph-paper representations can also be used.

$$\frac{1}{3} \quad + \quad \frac{2}{3} \quad = \quad 1 \qquad \textbf{or} \qquad \frac{1}{3} \quad + \quad \frac{1}{3} \quad + \quad \frac{1}{3} \quad = \quad 1$$

Once they are familiar with this procedure, students should explore ways in which one unit can be partitioned into fractional parts.

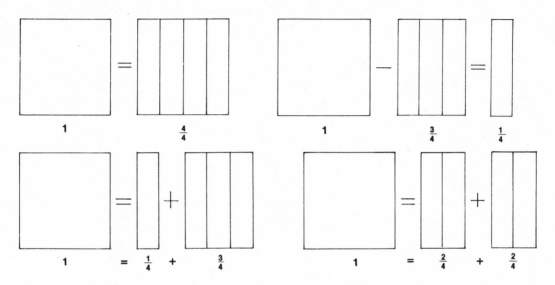

Have the students make up problems for each other. The results should be recorded in symbolic notation.

Activity 5-C3.
(symbolic)

• *Materials*   Fraction tiles, paper, pencils, Work Sheet 5-C3.

• ***Procedure***   Students are given problems such as

$$\frac{1}{3} + \frac{2}{3} = 1 \qquad\qquad \frac{2}{3} + \frac{1}{3} = 1 \qquad\qquad \frac{1}{3} + \frac{1}{3} = \frac{2}{3}$$
$$\frac{1}{3} + \frac{1}{3} + \frac{1}{3} = 1 \qquad\qquad \frac{2}{6} + \frac{3}{6} = \frac{5}{6}$$

If necessary, they may use fraction tiles or geoboards to validate the results. With sufficient practice—and reference to the fraction tiles as needed—similarities between operations with fractions and with whole numbers will be noted.

$$\frac{1}{3} + \frac{1}{3} = \frac{2}{3} \text{ is similar to } 1 + 1 = 2$$
$$\text{or } \frac{3}{4} - \frac{1}{4} = \frac{2}{4} \text{ is similar to } 3 - 1 = 2$$

Working with halves, thirds, and fourths, the students may predict the expected results for addition and subtraction of sixths, eighths, twelfths, etc. Have them use fraction tiles to validate their generalizations.

$$7 - 5 = 2 \text{ suggests } \frac{7}{12} - \frac{5}{12} = \frac{2}{12}$$
$$4 + 5 = 9 \text{ suggests } \frac{4}{8} + \frac{5}{8} = \frac{9}{8}$$

As they experiment with fraction tiles, students will discover other fraction relationships.

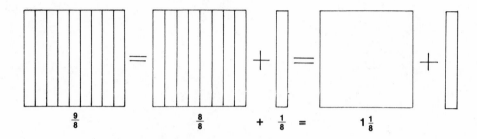

$$\frac{9}{8} \qquad \frac{8}{8} \qquad + \quad \frac{1}{8} \quad = \quad 1\frac{1}{8}$$

(Simplifying improper fractions)

Concept D: Addition and Subtraction of Fractions with Unlike Denominators

Activity 5-D1.
(concrete)

•*Materials*   Fraction tiles.

•*Procedure*   Ask the students to pick up the one-half and the one-fourth tiles.

$$\frac{1}{2} \qquad \frac{1}{4}$$ **(Symbols are for teacher reference only.)**

Name_____

Solve the problems below and write each letter above the correct answer to help you find the secret message at the bottom of the page. Use fraction titles if you need help.

1. $\frac{1}{2} + \frac{1}{2} = $ H

2. $\frac{1}{4} + \frac{1}{4} = $ V

3. $\frac{2}{4} + \frac{1}{4} = $ M

4. $\frac{3}{6} - \frac{1}{6} = $ T

5. $\frac{3}{8} + \frac{2}{8} = $ E

6. $\frac{6}{8} - \frac{3}{8} = $ N

7. $\frac{4}{12} + \frac{4}{12} + \frac{3}{12} = $ G

8. $\frac{4}{12} + \frac{5}{12} = $ A

9. $\frac{8}{12} - \frac{6}{12} = $ Y

10. $\frac{1}{2} - \frac{1}{4} = $ S

11. $\frac{6}{6} - \frac{2}{6} = $ R

Secret Message

___	___	___	H		___	___	___	___	___
$\frac{3}{4}$	$\frac{9}{12}$	$\frac{2}{6}$	$\frac{2}{2}$		$\frac{1}{4}$	$\frac{9}{12}$	$\frac{2}{4}$	$\frac{5}{8}$	$\frac{1}{4}$

___	___	___	___	___	___
$\frac{5}{8}$	$\frac{3}{8}$	$\frac{5}{8}$	$\frac{4}{6}$	$\frac{11}{12}$	$\frac{2}{12}$

Have them place the tiles next to each other.

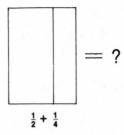

$$\frac{1}{2} + \frac{1}{4}$$

Since it is inconvenient to say "I have a one-half and a one-fourth tile," have the students place two one-fourth tiles on the one-half tile to determine equivalence.

$$\frac{1}{2} \qquad \frac{1}{4} + \frac{1}{4}$$

Encourage them to substitute the two one-fourth tiles for the one-half tile.

$$\frac{1}{2} + \frac{1}{4} \qquad \frac{1}{4} + \frac{1}{4} + \frac{1}{4} = \frac{3}{4}$$

Now by simply counting the pieces ("One fourth, two fourths, three fourths"), they will arrive at a more convenient manner of describing the sum: A one-half tile plus a one-fourth tile is a three-fourths tile.

$$\frac{1}{2} \quad + \quad \frac{1}{4} \quad = \quad \frac{3}{4}$$

As he is using concrete materials, the student does not need the numerals indicated in the figure in order to arrive at the solution. The use of symbols is not recommended at this level.

•*Materials*   Geoboards or dot paper, Work Sheet 5-D2.

Activity 5-D2.
(representational)

•***Procedure***   Have the children put red rubber bands around one half of the area of their geoboards.

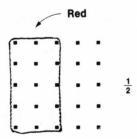

Red

$\frac{1}{2}$

Then have them put blue rubber bands around one fourth of their boards.

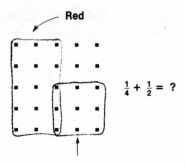

Ask how much of the geoboard is enclosed by both rubber bands. Again, they will find it inconvenient to say, "One-half plus one-fourth of the geoboard area is enclosed." By dividing the half into two fourths, the area can be determined by counting the fourths (blue regions).

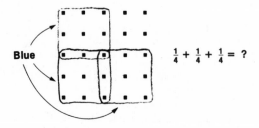

They will see that one half the area plus one fourth the area is three fourths of the geoboard area. (Recording the results using symbolic numerals is appropriate at this time.)

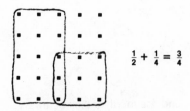

In order to model addition and subtraction of fractions, it is necessary to choose a unit of area on the geoboard which can be evenly partitioned into both fractional parts. For example, $\frac{1}{2} - \frac{1}{5}$ requires a unit area that can be evenly partitioned into halves and fifths. The unit below can be divided both into halves and into fifths. (Note: Each small square is one tenth.)

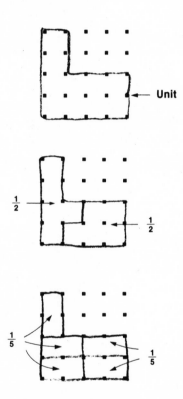

Therefore,

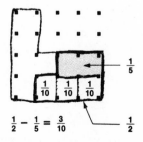

$$\frac{1}{2} - \frac{1}{5} = \frac{3}{10}$$

Name_____

On the geoboard dot patterns, show the fraction problems below
and fill in each answer.

Example:

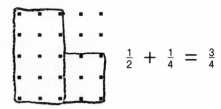

$\frac{1}{2} + \frac{1}{4} = \frac{3}{4}$

1. $\frac{3}{8} + \frac{1}{4} =$

2. $\frac{1}{2} - \frac{1}{8} =$

3. $\frac{1}{4} + \frac{5}{16} =$

4. $\frac{1}{3} + \frac{1}{4} =$

Many similar problems should be presented to students. The process of determining the unit area that will facilitate the solution is equivalent to finding the common denominator in the symbolic algorithm.

•*Materials*   Paper, pencils, Work Sheet 5-D3.

•***Procedure***   After extensive experience with Activity 5-D2, one of the following three algorithms can be presented along with appropriate explanations.

$$\frac{3}{4} + \frac{1}{6} = ?$$

A.
$$\frac{3}{4} \times \frac{3}{3} = \frac{9}{12}$$
$$+ \frac{1}{6} \times \frac{2}{2} = \frac{2}{12}$$
$$\overline{\frac{11}{12}}$$

B. $$\frac{3}{4} + \frac{1}{6} = \frac{(3 \times 6) + (4 \times 1)}{4 \times 6} = \frac{18 + 4}{24} = \frac{22}{24} = \frac{11}{12}$$

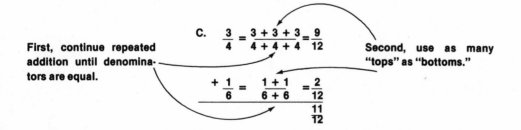

First, continue repeated addition until denominators are equal.

C. $$\frac{3}{4} = \frac{3+3+3}{4+4+4} = \frac{9}{12}$$
$$+ \frac{1}{6} = \frac{1+1}{6+6} = \frac{2}{12}$$
$$\overline{\frac{11}{12}}$$

Second, use as many "tops" as "bottoms."

Allow validation with fraction tiles or geoboards as necessary.

Name_____

Solve the problems below using your favorite method. The letter
next to each problem can be placed over the correct fraction at
the bottom of the page to uncover the secret message.

1. $\dfrac{1}{3}$ **2.** $\dfrac{1}{6}$ **3.** $\dfrac{1}{3}$ **4.** $\dfrac{3}{4}$ **5.** $\dfrac{4}{12}$

$+\dfrac{1}{2}$ $+\dfrac{3}{4}$ $+\dfrac{1}{6}$ $-\dfrac{1}{2}$ $+\dfrac{1}{4}$

  U   I   N   R   H

6. $\dfrac{1}{4} + \dfrac{3}{8} = $ G

7. $\dfrac{5}{12} - \dfrac{1}{3} = $ T

8. $\dfrac{3}{8} + \dfrac{1}{6} = $ K

9. $\dfrac{3}{5} + \dfrac{1}{4} = $ S

Secret Message

$\overline{}$ $\overline{}$ $\overline{}$ $\overline{}$ $\overline{}$ $\overline{}$ $\overline{}$ $\overline{}$

$\dfrac{1}{12}$ $\dfrac{7}{12}$ $\dfrac{11}{12}$ $\dfrac{3}{6}$ $\dfrac{13}{24}$ $\dfrac{11}{12}$ $\dfrac{3}{6}$ $\dfrac{5}{8}$

$\overline{}$ $\overset{U}{\overline{}}$ $\overline{}$ $\overline{}$ $\overline{}$

$\dfrac{7}{12}$ $\dfrac{5}{6}$ $\dfrac{1}{4}$ $\dfrac{1}{12}$ $\dfrac{17}{20}$

Concept E: Fraction Multiplication

•*Materials*   Fraction tiles.

Note: The concept of fraction multiplication may first be introduced as an extension of the concept of fractional part. For example, half of twenty peanuts is ten peanuts can be represented as $\frac{1}{2} \times 20 = 10$. We will consider only problems in which both factors are numbers between zero and one, though these techniques can be extended to more complicated situations. Fraction tiles constructed out of colored translucent acetate sheets will facilitate the understanding of this concept.

•***Procedure***   Have the students choose two fraction tiles and overlap them as pictured below.

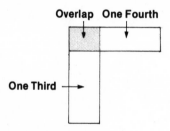

Lay the above configuration on a clear unit square and determine the fractional part of the unit square accounted for by the overlapped portion.

One Twelfth of Total Area

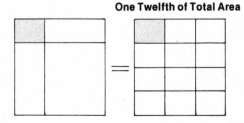

At this stage, it is not necessary to define the concept symbolically (i.e., $\frac{1}{4} \times \frac{1}{3} = \frac{1}{12}$). Students should work out several examples similar to the one above.

Activity 5-E2.
(representational)

•*Materials*   Pencils, Work Sheet 5-E2.

•***Procedure***   To find half of two thirds (i.e., $\frac{1}{2} \times \frac{2}{3} = ?$), have students mark off the top edge of a square in thirds and the left edge in halves.

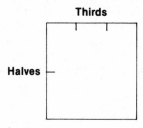

They should divide the square into equal parts by completing the grid

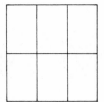

and indicate the number of halves and thirds on each axis with a bracket.

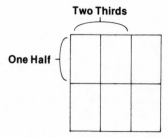

To determine one half of two thirds, they need only shade in the rectangle enclosed by both brackets

Name_____

Use the squares below to solve the fraction-multiplication problems.

Example:

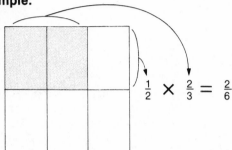

$\frac{1}{2}$ ✕ $\frac{2}{3}$ = $\frac{2}{6}$

1.

$\frac{1}{4}$ ✕ $\frac{1}{3}$ =

2.

$\frac{1}{2}$ ✕ $\frac{1}{5}$ =

3.

$\frac{2}{3}$ ✕ $\frac{3}{4}$ =

4.

$\frac{2}{3}$ ✕ $\frac{1}{6}$ =

5.

$\frac{3}{5}$ ✕ $\frac{2}{6}$ =

6.

$\frac{3}{4}$ ✕ $\frac{3}{8}$ =

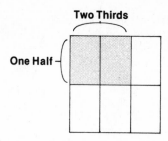

and then find what fractional part it is of the whole. Since each small rectangle is one sixth of the whole square, the shaded area is two sixths. Therefore, one half of two thirds is two sixths. Note that the vertical lines divide the square into thirds and that the horizontal line divides each third in half, thereby providing a model for this type of problem.

The solution for two fifths of five sixths is pictured as follows:

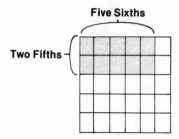

Two fifths of five sixths is ten thirtieths (i.e., $\frac{2}{5} \times \frac{5}{6} = \frac{10}{30}$). The answer can be reduced by means of techniques developed in Activity 5-B3, though it is not recommended at this time. Encourage students to make up problems for one another and to record their results using symbolic notation.

Activity 5-E3.
(symbolic)

•*Materials*   Paper, pencils, Work Sheet 5-E3.

•***Procedure***   The following algorithm should be introduced after students have had extensive experience with Activities 5-E1 and 5-E2. Don't be surprised if the students discover the algorithm for themselves.

$$\frac{4}{5} \times \frac{3}{4} = \frac{4 \times 3}{5 \times 4} = \frac{12}{20}$$

Note that the fraction algorithm above is based on whole-number operations. Initially, little concern should be paid to reducing answers since it only confuses the fraction concepts and since in any case it is questionable whether the reduced fraction is really simpler to think about than the original.

Name_____

Solve the following problems, placing each letter above the correct answer at the bottom of the page to find the secret message. (Answers should be reduced.)

1. $\frac{2}{3} \times \frac{3}{4} = P$

2. $\frac{2}{5} \times \frac{2}{3} = O$

3. $\frac{1}{4} \times \frac{1}{2} = B$

4. $\frac{5}{8} \times \frac{1}{3} = R$

5. $\frac{5}{6} \times \frac{2}{5} = E$

6. $\frac{3}{12} \times \frac{2}{3} = H$

7. $\frac{3}{8} \times \frac{3}{4} = I$

8. $\frac{6}{10} \times \frac{2}{3} = G$

9. $\frac{3}{8} \times \frac{6}{12} = N$

Secret Message

$$\underline{\quad} \quad \underline{\quad} \quad \underline{\quad} \qquad\qquad \underline{\quad} \quad \underline{\quad} \quad \underline{\quad} \quad \underline{\quad} \quad \underline{\quad}$$
$$\frac{1}{8} \qquad \frac{9}{32} \qquad \frac{2}{5} \qquad\qquad \frac{2}{5}\text{-} \qquad \frac{5}{24} \qquad \frac{1}{3} \qquad \frac{1}{3} \qquad \frac{3}{16}$$

$$\underline{\quad P \quad} \qquad \underline{\quad} \qquad \underline{\quad} \qquad\qquad \underline{\quad} \qquad\qquad \underline{\quad}$$
$$\frac{1}{2} \qquad\quad \frac{1}{6} \qquad\quad \frac{5}{24} \qquad\qquad \frac{4}{15} \qquad\qquad \frac{2}{5}$$

From *Mathmatters*, copyright © 1978 by Goodyear Publishing Company, Inc.

Concept F: Fraction Division

Activity 5-F1.
(concrete)

• *Materials*   Fraction tiles.

• *Procedure*   In order to build a conceptual basis for fraction division, we will use the familiar concept of whole-number division. Have the students choose one fraction tile (say a tile representing one half) and see how many one eighth tiles will fit onto it.

One Half

One Eighth

They will find that four one-eighth tiles are required to cover a one-half tile completely.

Continue this process with additional problems, making sure that the examples posed have whole-number solutions (i.e., that the covering process comes out even). For example,

1. $\frac{1}{2} \div \frac{1}{4} = ?$

2. $\frac{1}{3} \div \frac{1}{6} = ?$

3. $\frac{2}{3} \div \frac{1}{6} = ?$

When the teacher poses problems, he should refer to the fraction tiles by color, not by their associated symbolic notation. Hence, when posing a problem such as the three listed above, he should ask, "How many blues are needed to cover a red?"

Activity 5-F2.
(representational)

• *Materials*   Geoboards or dot paper, Work Sheet 5-F2.

• *Procedure*   With the whole geoboard designated as the unit (one), have each student put a rubber band around three fourths. At this point, recording with symbolic fractions should be encouraged.

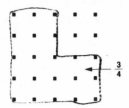

To solve $\frac{3}{4} \div \frac{1}{4}$, students must simply determine how many fourths are in three fourths.

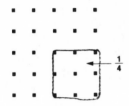

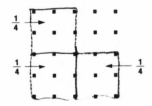

They will discover that there are three one fourths in three fourths. Therefore,

$$\frac{3}{4} \div \frac{1}{4} = 3$$

Note the similarity between the concepts of whole-number division and fraction division. Several problems of this type should be experienced ($\frac{2}{4} \div \frac{1}{4}$, $\frac{4}{10} \div \frac{2}{10}$, $\frac{5}{6} \div \frac{1}{6}$, etc.). Unlike denominators should be changed to like denominators by means of techniques introduced earlier (see 5-B3 and 5-B4). For example,

1. $\frac{1}{2} \div \frac{1}{4} = \frac{2}{4} \div \frac{1}{4} = ?$

2. $\frac{3}{5} \div \frac{3}{10} = \frac{6}{10} \div \frac{3}{10} = ?$

Only problems that provide whole-number answers should be utilized at this level.

Name_____

Solve the following fraction-division problems by using the geoboard dot patterns below.

Example:

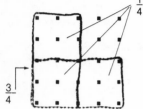

$$\frac{3}{4} \div \frac{1}{4} = 3$$

1.

$$\frac{2}{4} \div \frac{1}{4} =$$

2.

$$\frac{5}{8} \div \frac{1}{8} =$$

3.

$$\frac{6}{16} \div \frac{2}{16} =$$

4.

$$\frac{6}{8} \div \frac{1}{4} =$$

5.

$$\frac{8}{16} \div \frac{1}{4} =$$

6.

$$\frac{10}{16} \div \frac{1}{8} =$$

• *Materials*   Paper, pencils, Work Sheet 5-F3.

• **Procedure**   After students have had extensive experience with activities 5-F1 and 5-F2, the following algorithms should be introduced with appropriate explanation.

Common Denominator Method: $\dfrac{a}{c} \div \dfrac{b}{c} = a \div b = \dfrac{a}{b}$

Examples:

1. $\dfrac{3}{4} \div \dfrac{1}{4} = 3 \div 1 = 3$

2. $\dfrac{4}{5} \div \dfrac{3}{5} = 4 \div 3 = \dfrac{4}{3}$

3. $\dfrac{4}{6} \div \dfrac{1}{3} = \dfrac{4}{6} \div \dfrac{2}{6} = 4 \div 2 = 2$

Traditional Method: $\dfrac{a}{c} \div \dfrac{b}{d} = \dfrac{a}{c} \times \dfrac{d}{b} = \dfrac{a \times d}{c \times b}$

Examples:

1. $\dfrac{3}{4} \div \dfrac{1}{4} = \dfrac{3}{4} \times \dfrac{4}{1} = \dfrac{3 \times 4}{4 \times 1} = \dfrac{12}{4} = 3$

2. $\dfrac{4}{5} \div \dfrac{3}{5} = \dfrac{4}{5} \times \dfrac{5}{3} = \dfrac{4 \times 5}{5 \times 3} = \dfrac{20}{15} = \dfrac{4}{3}$

3. $\dfrac{4}{6} \div \dfrac{1}{3} = \dfrac{4}{6} \times \dfrac{3}{1} = \dfrac{4 \times 3}{6 \times 1} = \dfrac{12}{6} = 2$

Problems with fraction solutions should be introduced at the symbolic level since little conceptual benefit is derived from introducing them earlier. Students can in fact experience considerable confusion if fractional quotients are introduced at the concrete level.

Name_____

Solve the following problems, placing each letter above the correct answer at the bottom of the page to find the secret message.
(Answers should be reduced.)

1. $\frac{2}{3} \div \frac{1}{2} = $ D

2. $\frac{3}{4} \div \frac{1}{5} = $ N

3. $\frac{5}{8} \div \frac{1}{3} = $ U

4. $\frac{7}{12} \div \frac{1}{2} = $ R

5. $\frac{5}{6} \div \frac{2}{3} = $ E

6. $\frac{9}{16} \div \frac{3}{4} = $ O

Secret Message

$\underline{}$ $\underline{}$ $\overset{\text{D}}{\underline{}}$ $\underline{}$ $\underline{}$ $\underline{}$

$\frac{15}{8}$ $\frac{7}{6}$ $\frac{4}{3}$ $\frac{3}{4}$ $\frac{15}{4}$ $\frac{5}{4}$

Notes for Topic 5

Operations with Decimals

In order to introduce decimal fractions effectively, one must first demonstrate to students why such fractions are necessary at all. The decimal point and decimal fractions are used merely as communication aids. When we allow the unit to vary freely, there is no need for a decimal point. For example, if we measured the length of a telephone receiver in centimeters and found it to be 20.5 centimeters long, we might conclude that decimals are necessary for accuracy. However, by changing the unit of measurement to millimeters, we would arrive at an equally accurate measure of 205 millimeters and would not require the use of decimal fractions.

It is tedious and unprofitable, though, to attempt to eliminate fractional parts by changing the size of the unit. In some cases—decimal division, for example—it is convenient to change the size of the unit by moving the decimal point in the divisor and the dividend. In most cases, however, it is more convenient to use fractional parts of the unit.

There is no way to avoid the issue. Sometimes smaller pieces are needed (as in measurement), sometimes greater accuracy (as in money transactions). With the growing use of two new mathematical tools in the classroom—handheld calculators and metric measurement—decimal fractions become increasingly more useful than ratio fractions. The relevance of studying thirds, quarters, eighths, twelfths, sixteenths, etc., will diminish as ounces and pounds; cups, pints, quarts, and gallons; and inches, feet, yards, and miles are replaced by grams, liters, and meters, all based on the same decimal notation. As calculators make the extensive manipulation of multidigit numbers possible for all students, an understanding of the nature of decimal fractions and the placement of the decimal point becomes an essential key to other worlds of mathematical exploration.

Concept A: Special Fractions

Activity 6-A1.
(concrete)

•*Materials*   A set of Base-ten blocks or similar items are necessary to provide efficient concrete experience with fractional parts as small as $\frac{1}{1000}$ (see Appendix 3).

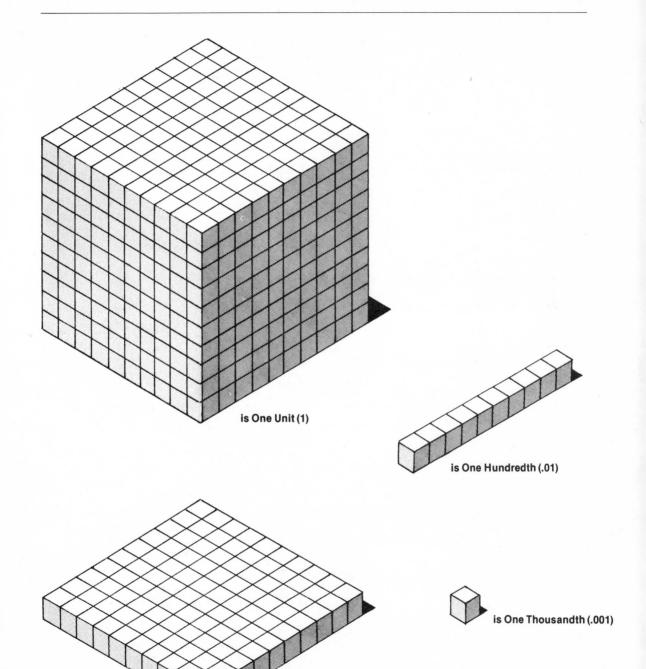

is One Unit (1)

is One Hundredth (.01)

is One Tenth (.1)

is One Thousandth (.001)

•*Procedure*   Have students use these blocks to solve the following problems. It is not necessary to make symbolic recordings of the results at this time. Students should, however, be encouraged to make verbalizations such as, "A tenth block and a tenth block make two tenth blocks."
How much do you have here?

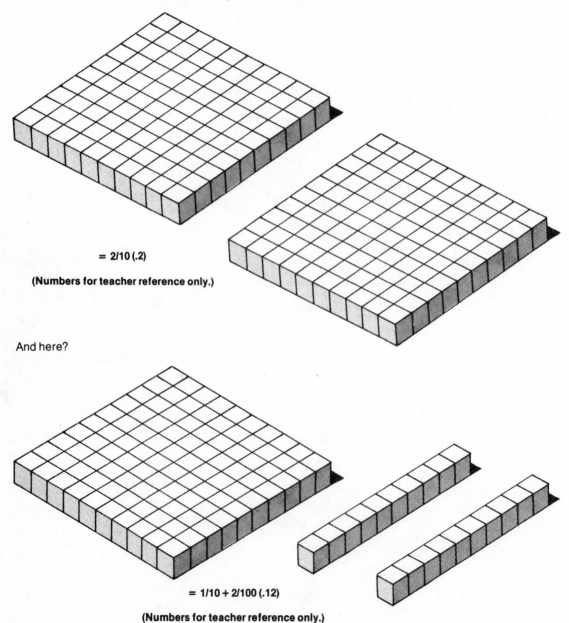

= 2/10 (.2)

(Numbers for teacher reference only.)

And here?

= 1/10 + 2/100 (.12)

(Numbers for teacher reference only.)

And here?

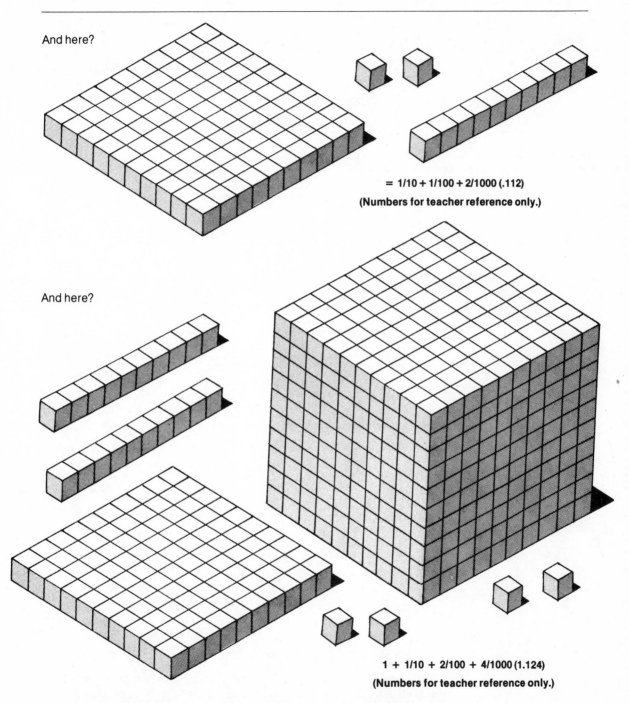

= 1/10 + 1/100 + 2/1000 (.112)

(Numbers for teacher reference only.)

And here?

1 + 1/10 + 2/100 + 4/1000 (1.124)

(Numbers for teacher reference only.)

Have the children make up problems of their own and verbalize the solutions.

Activity 6-A2.
(representational)

•*Materials*   Paper, pencils, Work Sheet 6-A2.

•*Procedure*   If our representational notation is to accommodate use of decimals, it must be expanded to include cubes as well as squares, lines, and dots. We will assign values in the following manner:

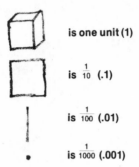

is one unit (1)

is $\frac{1}{10}$ (.1)

is $\frac{1}{100}$ (.01)

is $\frac{1}{1000}$ (.001)

Devise problems similar to those in the previous activity. As students begin to record their results, introduce them to decimal notation. How much do you have here?

How much do you have here?

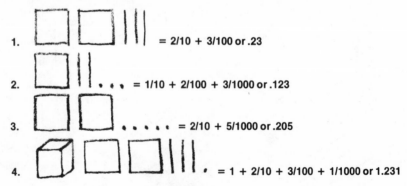

1. = 2/10 + 3/100 or .23

2. = 1/10 + 2/100 + 3/1000 or .123

3. = 2/10 + 5/1000 or .205

4. = 1 + 2/10 + 3/100 + 1/1000 or 1.231

It is important to explain to your students that decimal notation eliminates the need for denominators by assigning values of tenths, hundredths, and thousandths to the places to the right of the decimal point. The decimal point indicates where the fractional values begin.

Name_____

Use numerals to name these fractions.

Example:

□ □ ▌▌▌ = $\frac{2}{10}$ + $\frac{3}{100}$

1. □ ▌▌ ••• =

2. □ □ ••••• =

3. ▦ □ □ ▌▌▌ • =

4. ▦ ▦ ▌▌▌ =

5. ▌▌ ••••••• =

6. □ □ □ □ ▌ ••••••• =

7. ▦ ▦ ▦ •••• =

From *Mathmatters*, copyright © 1978 by Goodyear Publishing Company, Inc.

Activity 6-A3.
(symbolic)

•*Materials*   Paper, pencils, Work Sheet 6-A3.

•**Procedure**   Have students solve the following problems by filling in the grids.

1. $1/10 + 2/100 =$

$\frac{1}{10}$	$\frac{1}{100}$	$\frac{1}{1000}$
1	2	0

2. $2/10 + 3/100 + 7/1000 =$

$\frac{1}{10}$	$\frac{1}{100}$	$\frac{1}{1000}$
2	3	7

3. $5/10 + 3/1000 =$

$\frac{1}{10}$	$\frac{1}{100}$	$\frac{1}{1000}$
5	0	3

Note that all numerators are less than ten. In the next section, we will investigate the necessity of regrouping when numerators are greater than ten.

WORK SHEET 6-A3

Name_____

Record these fractions on the place-value grids.

Example:

$\frac{1}{10} + \frac{2}{100} =$

1		$\frac{1}{10}$	$\frac{1}{100}$	$\frac{1}{1000}$
.		1	2	0

1		$\frac{1}{10}$	$\frac{1}{100}$	$\frac{1}{1000}$

1. $\frac{2}{10} + \frac{3}{100} + \frac{7}{1000} =$

2. $\frac{5}{10} + \frac{3}{1000} =$

3. $6 + \frac{3}{10} + \frac{8}{100} + \frac{5}{1000}$

4. $4 + \frac{9}{100}$

5. $\frac{7}{100}$

6. $3 + \frac{8}{1000}$

7. $\frac{4}{1000}$

From *Mathmatters*, copyright © 1978 by Goodyear Publishing Company, Inc.

Concept B: Addition of Decimal Fractions

Activity 6-B1.
(concrete)

●*Materials*   A set of base-ten blocks or similar materials.

●*Procedure*   Set up the following problem and have students find the solution.

.124

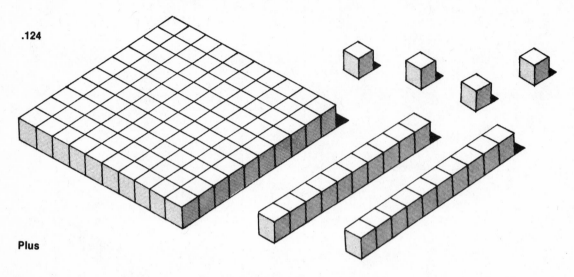

Plus

.132

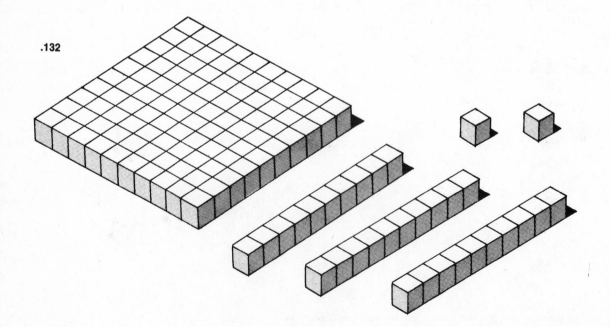

Equals

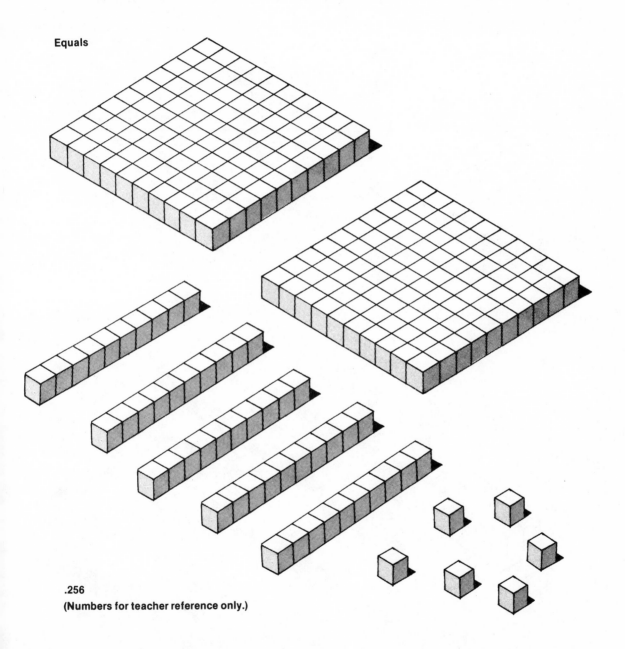

.256
(Numbers for teacher reference only.)

Ask students to perform the following addition problem, attending to place-value regrouping.

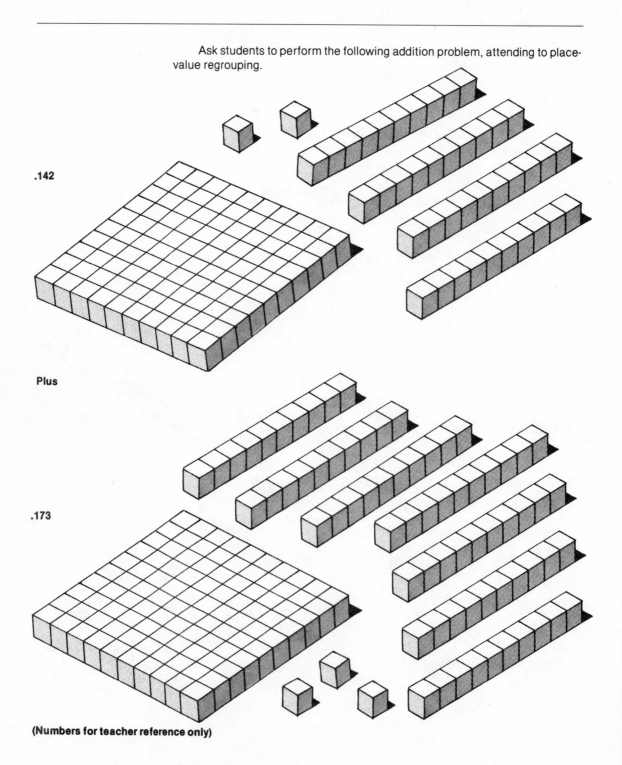

.142

Plus

.173

(Numbers for teacher reference only)

equals

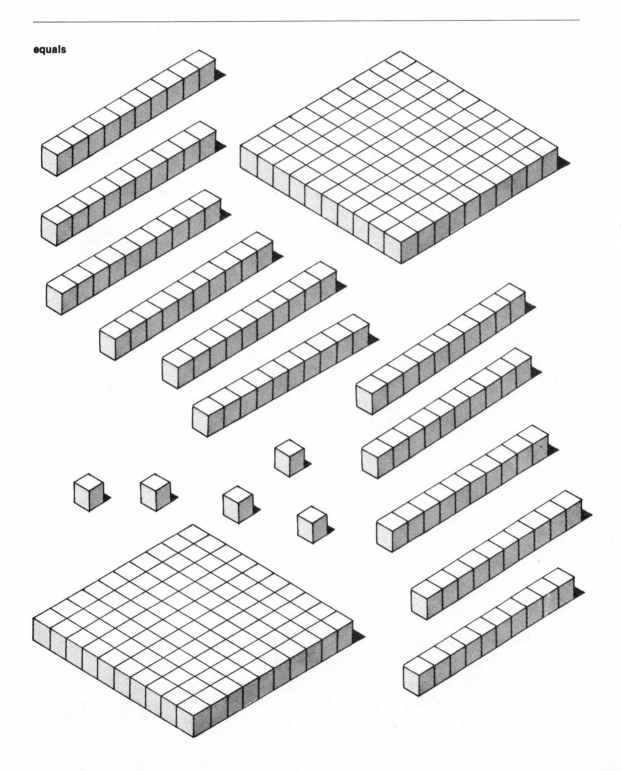

After regrouping we have:

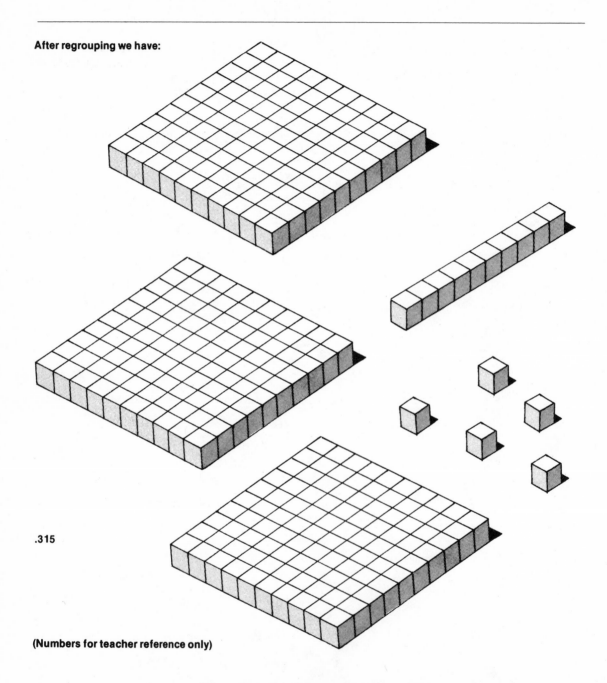

.315

(Numbers for teacher reference only)

    Regrouping with decimal fractions is similar to regrouping with whole numbers. It is only the decimal point that identifies the above exercise as a fraction problem. Have students set up similar problems for each other to solve.

•*Materials*   Paper, pencils, Work Sheet 6-B2.

Activity 6-B2.
(representational)

•***Procedure***   Have students solve the following problems by means of representational notation. Ask them to record the results in both representational and symbolic notation.

1.

	$\frac{1}{10}$	$\frac{1}{100}$	$\frac{1}{1000}$
.	2	2	3
+.	3	2	2
.	5	4	5

2.

	$\frac{1}{10}$	$\frac{1}{100}$	$\frac{1}{1000}$	
.	2	5	8	
+.	1	2	4	
.	3	7	12	⟩ Regroup
.	3	8	2	

3.

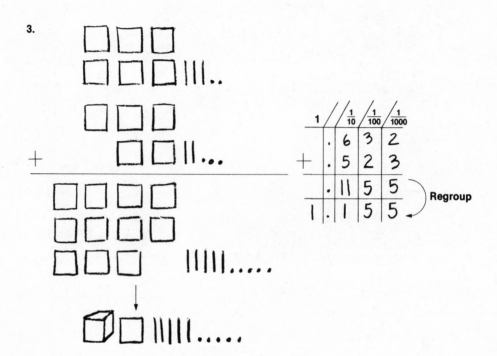

Note the use of the grid as an aid in the regrouping process.

Name_____

Solve these problems.

Examples:

	1			$\frac{1}{10}$	$\frac{1}{100}$	$\frac{1}{1000}$

A.

			.	2	2	3
+		+	.	3	2	2
			.	5	4	5

B.

			.	2	5	8
+		+	.	1	2	4
			.	3	7	12
			.	3	8	2

1.

			.	2	3	6
+		+	.	5	2	3

2.

			.	4	7	5
+		+	.	3	3	8

3.

		1	.	2	5	9
+		+ 3	.	3	0	6

4.

		3	.	0	0	8
+		+ 2	.	0	0	3

Activity 6-B3.
(symbolic)

•*Materials*   Paper, pencils, Work Sheet 6-B3.

•*Procedure*   Teach the addition algorithm for decimal fractions. The following problems can be solved by means of techniques similar to those taught for whole-number addition.

.24 + .315 =

or

.2 4 0
+ .3 1 5
———
.5 5 5

	$\frac{1}{10}$	$\frac{1}{100}$	$\frac{1}{1000}$
.	2	4	0
+.	3	1	5
.	5	5	5

.256 + .175 =

or

.2 5 6
+ .1 7 5
———
.4 3 1

	$\frac{1}{10}$	$\frac{1}{100}$	$\frac{1}{1000}$	
.	2	5	6	
+.	1	7	5	
.	3	12	11	⟩ Regroup
.	3	13	1	⟩ Regroup
.	4	3	1	

Decimal-fraction addition is much easier than regular-fraction addition because there is no need to establish common denominators. In the place-value system, every denominator is a multiple of ten.

Name_____

Solve these problems.

	1	$\frac{1}{10}$	$\frac{1}{100}$	$\frac{1}{1000}$

Example:

$$.24 + .315 = \begin{array}{r} .240 \\ +\underline{.315} \\ .555 \end{array}$$

.	2	4	
.	3	1	5
.	5	5	5

1.

$$.256 + .175 = \begin{array}{r} .256 \\ +\underline{.175} \end{array}$$

| . | 2 | 5 | 6 |
| . | 1 | 7 | 5 |

2. $3.709 + 1.222 = \begin{array}{r} 3.709 \\ +\underline{1.222} \end{array}$

3. $4.068 + 3.125$

4. $.007 + 1.995$

5. $6.42 + 8.525$

6. $.068 + .073$

Concept C: Subtraction of Decimal Fractions

Activity 6-C1.
(concrete)

•*Materials* A set of base-ten blocks or similar materials.

•***Procedure*** Concrete materials are used to set up and solve the following problem.

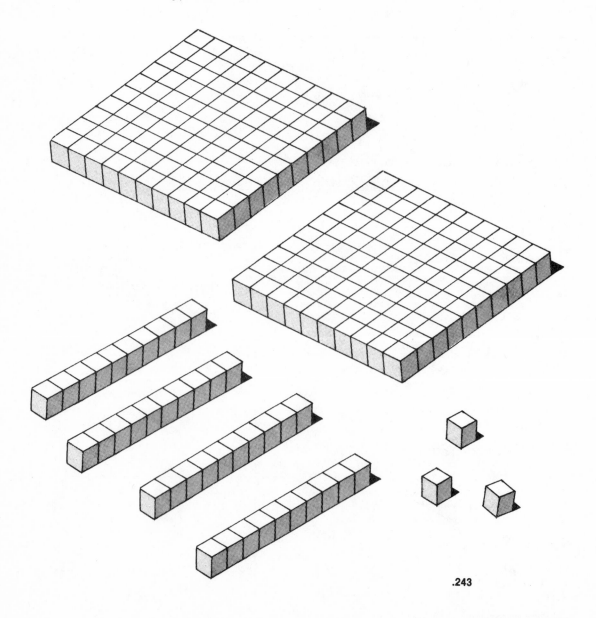

.243

Minus

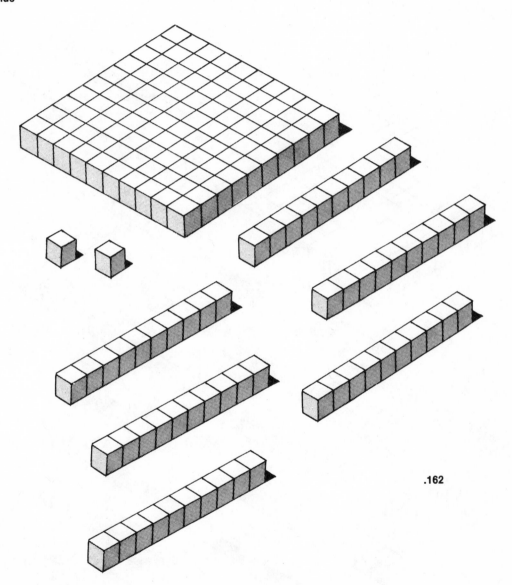

.162

Students will recognize that they cannot take six rods (.06) away from the first group of blocks unless they regroup one of the flats (.1) into ten rods (.10). Therefore the problem becomes:

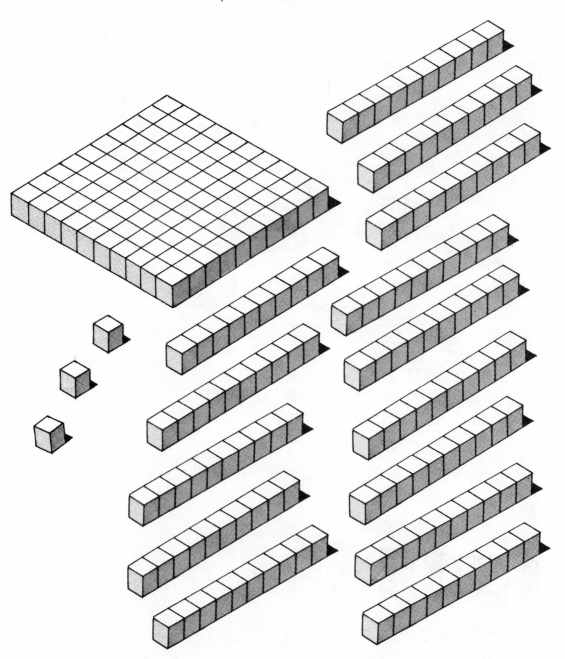

Minus

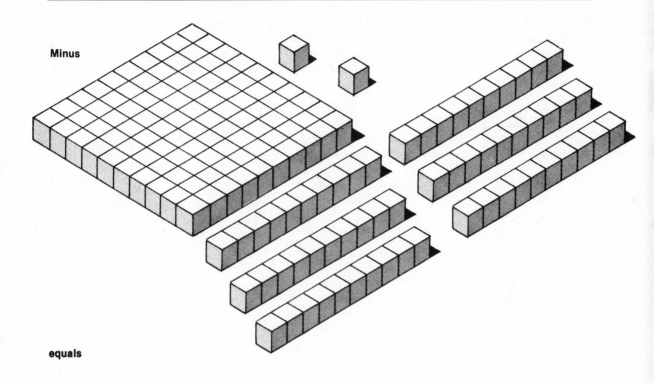

equals

Have the students make up problems with and without regrouping. Do not re-quire recording of results with symbolic notation at this time.

Activity 6-C2.
(representational)

•*Materials*   Paper, pencils, Work Sheet 6-C2.

•*Procedure*   Have students use representational notation to solve the following problem, recording the results in both representational and symbolic notation.

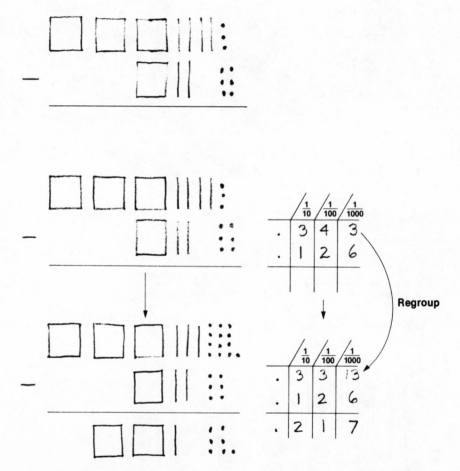

Name_____

Solve these subtraction problems.

Example:

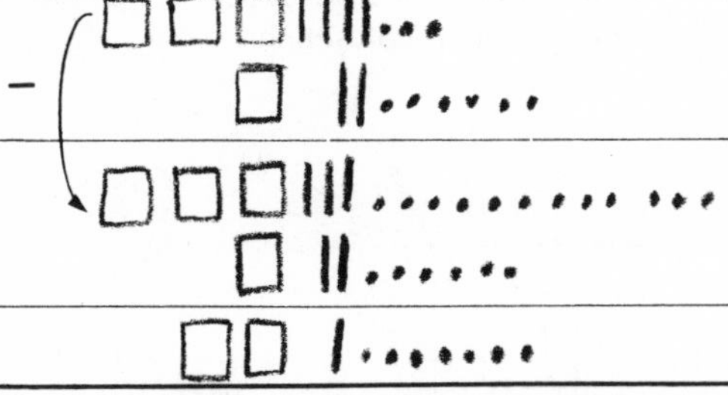

	1		$\frac{1}{10}$	$\frac{1}{100}$	$\frac{1}{1000}$	
−		.	3	4	3	⎞ Regroup
−		.	1	2	6	⎠
		.	3	3	13	
		.	1	2	6	
		.	2	1	7	

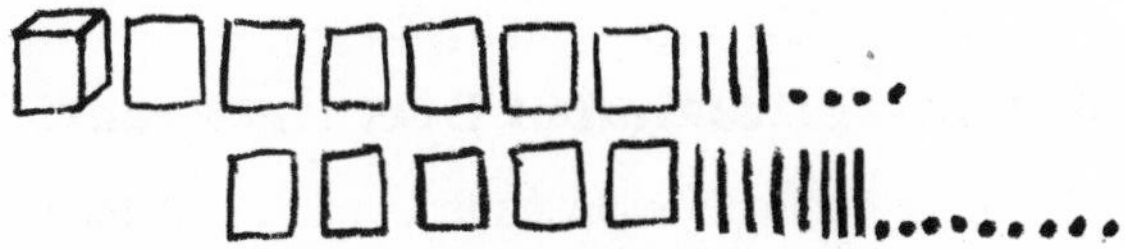

1.

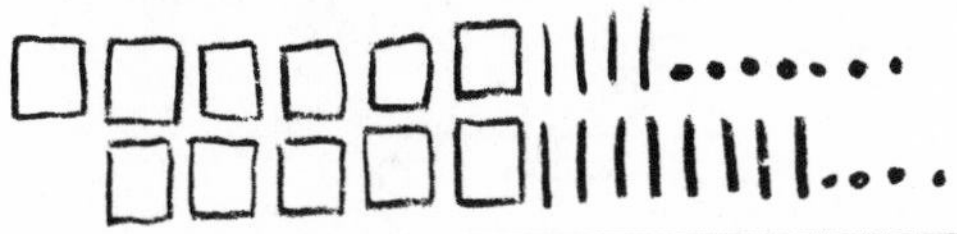

		.	6	4	7
−		.	5	8	4

2.

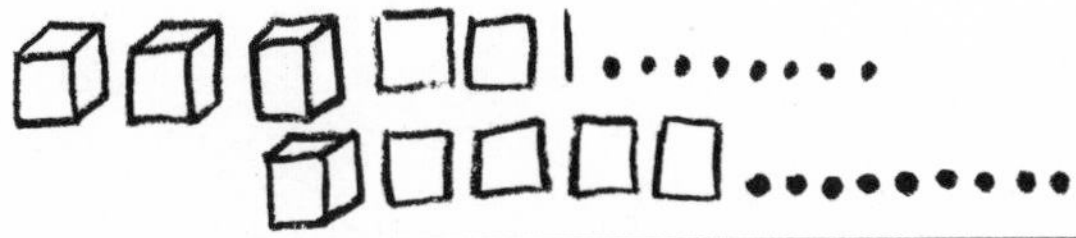

	3	.	2	1	8
−	1	.	4	0	9

3.

	1	.	6	3	4
−		.	5	8	9

4.

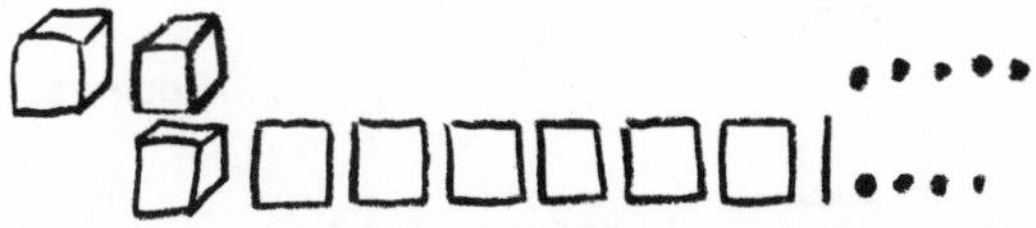

	2	.	0	0	5
−	1	.	6	1	4

Activity 6-C3.
(symbolic)

•*Materials*   Paper, pencils, Work Sheet 6-C3.

•***Procedure***   In order to acquaint students with the decimal-fraction subtraction algorithm, guide them in solving the following problems, using techniques similar to those taught for whole-number subtraction.

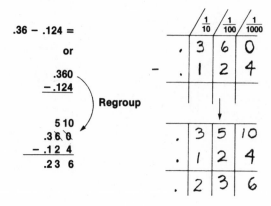

$.36 - .124 =$

or

.360
−.124

Regroup

```
  5 10
.3 6 0
−.1 2 4
 .2 3 6
```

Concept D: Multiplication of Decimal Fractions

Activity 6-D1.
(concrete)

•*Materials*   To model decimal multiplication, you need a ten-by-ten-inch paper grid and colored squares that exactly fit each square in the grid.

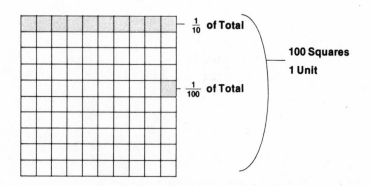

$\frac{1}{10}$ of Total

$\frac{1}{100}$ of Total

100 Squares
1 Unit

Name_____

Solve these subtraction problems.

Example:

	1		$\frac{1}{10}$	$\frac{1}{100}$	$\frac{1}{1000}$	

.36 − .124 = .3 6 0
　　　　− .1 2 4

| | . | 3 | 6 | 0 |
| − | . | 1 | 2 | 4 |

　　　　　 5　10
　　　.3 6̸ 0̸
　　　.1 2 4
　　　.2 3 6

.	3	5	10
.	1	2	4
.	2	3	6

1.　　.465 − .368 = .465
　　　　　　　−.368

| | . | 4 | 6 | 5 |
| − | . | 3 | 6 | 8 |

2.　　1.206 − .625 = 1.206
　　　　　　　　−.625

3.　　.831 − .813 = .831
　　　　　　　−.813

4.　　1.094 − .98 = 1.094
　　　　　　　− .98

•**Procedure** Have the students multiply decimal fractions in the following manner.

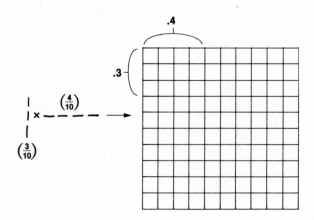

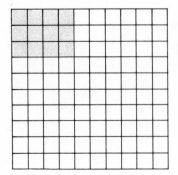

Place colored squares on the appropriate part of the grid to form a rectangle.

Since the rectangle covers twelve of the hundred squares,

$$\frac{3}{10} \times \frac{4}{10} = \frac{12}{100}$$

or

$$.3 \times .4 = .12$$

This procedure works with hundredths and thousandths, but such problems would be very time consuming. Hence, though the exercise is valuable as an introduction to decimal multiplication in that it shows the similarity between regular-fraction and decimal-fraction multiplication, it is not a useful model for problems involving smaller fractions. More complicated decimal fractions are better handled at the symbolic level.

•*Materials*   Graph paper, pencils, Work Sheet 6-D2.

•***Procedure***   Follow the same procedure as outlined in Activity 6-D1, but in place of the grid and colored squares, simply color in the squares on graph paper.

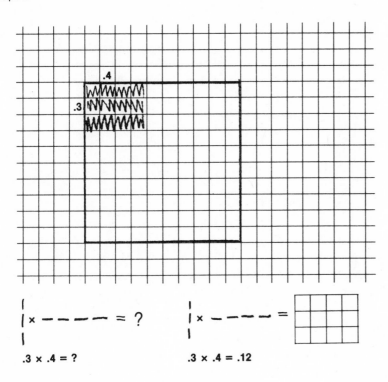

.3 × .4 = ?

.3 × .4 = .12

Point out to students that when you multiply tenths, you get hundredths. If you multiply tenths by hundredths, what would you get? Encourage them to discover a pattern.

•*Materials*   Paper, pencils, Work Sheet 6-D3.

•***Procedure***   Teach the decimal-fraction multiplication algorithm. In order to place the decimal point in the proper place, it is necessary that students consider the product of the denominator in each decimal fraction.

$.6 \times .24 = \frac{6}{10} \times \frac{24}{100}$

Name_____

Solve these multiplication problems.

Example

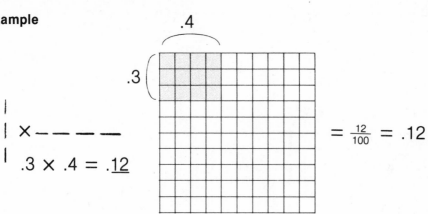

$= \frac{12}{100} = .12$

| × — — — —
| .3 × .4 = .<u>12</u>

1.

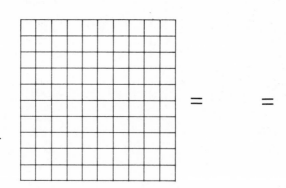

| × — — — —
| .6 × .5 = ____

$=$ $=$

2.

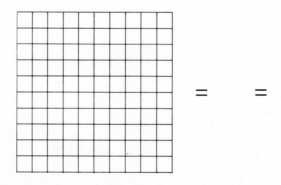

| × — — — —
| .8 × .4 = ____

$=$ $=$

3. .7 × .6 = ____   **4.** .4 × .9 = ____   **5.** .25 × .2 = ____

From *Mathmatters*, copyright © 1978 by Goodyear Publishing Company, Inc.

The answer will require that the last digit be in the $\frac{1}{10}$ × $\frac{1}{100}$, or ($\frac{1}{1000}$), place. Therefore,

$$\begin{array}{r} .\ 24 \\ \times\ .\ \ 6 \\ \hline .144 \end{array}$$

Tell students that an easy way to determine where to place the decimal point is to total the number of digits to the right of the decimal point in both the multiplier and the multiplicand (2 + 1 = 3, in this case). The answer will re-quire that same number of digits to the right of the decimal point.

$$\begin{array}{r} .\ 25 \\ \times\ .\ \ 3 \\ \hline .075 \end{array}$$

It is important that students recognize the similarity between whole-number and decimal-fraction multiplication. The placement of the decimal point is the primary distinction.

Concept E: Division of Decimal Fractions

•*Materials*   A ten-by-ten-inch paper grid and colored squares that exactly fit each square in the grid.

Activity 6-E1.
(concrete)

•*Procedure*   To teach them to divide .6 by .2, have students observe the following:

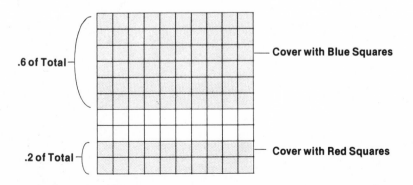

.6 of Total — ——— Cover with Blue Squares

.2 of Total — ——— Cover with Red Squares

Ask them how many times the red area (.2) will fit into the blue area (.6). After students solve this problem, continue to present them with similar problems carefully selected to have no remainder.

Name_____

Solve these multiplication problems.

Example:

$$
\begin{array}{r}
.24 \\
\times\ .6 \\
\hline
.144
\end{array}
\qquad
\frac{6}{10} \ \times\ \frac{24}{100} \ =\ \frac{6 \times 24}{1000} \ =\ \frac{144}{1000} \ =\ .144
$$

1.
$$
\begin{array}{r}
.25 \\
\times\ .3 \\
\hline
\end{array}
$$

2.
$$
\begin{array}{r}
.68 \\
\times\ .5 \\
\hline
\end{array}
$$

3.
$$
\begin{array}{r}
.7 \\
\times\ .43 \\
\hline
\end{array}
$$

4.
$$
\begin{array}{r}
.30 \\
\times\ .45 \\
\hline
\end{array}
$$

5.
$$
\begin{array}{r}
.95 \\
\times\ .64 \\
\hline
\end{array}
$$

Division of decimal fractions is primarily a symbolic operation. It is difficult, at best, to provide physical modeling of the process with any but the simplest of decimal fractions. We are confronted with the same inadequacies that we encountered when developing models to demonstrate regular fraction division, and the situation is somewhat further complicated by the minuteness of the fractions ($\frac{1}{10}$, $\frac{1}{100}$, $\frac{1}{1000}$) and the large grids that are therefore necessary for modeling decimal division. Though simple examples can be explored in a concrete manner, it is our conclusion that decimal division is most efficiently experienced at the symbolic level if it is introduced as a natural extension of whole-number division. The conceptual model illustrated above is identical to that of regular-fraction division. This situation provides an excellent example of the immense power of the symbolic notation utilized in mathematics. The student should come to appreciate the power of algorithms and to use them not out of fear but out of informed choice.

•*Materials*   Graph paper, pencils, Work Sheet 6-E2.

•***Procedure***   Follow the same procedure as in Activity 6-E1 but this time color in the rectangles on graph paper.

Activity 6-E2.
(representational)

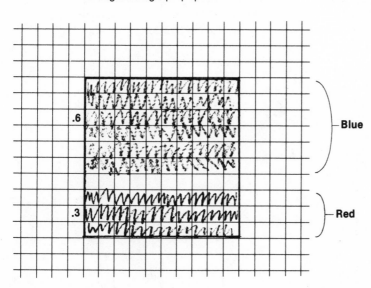

Blue

Red

How many times will the red area exactly fit into the blue area?

.6 ÷ .3 = 2

or $.3\overline{)\,.6}^{\,2}$

Name_____

Solve these division problems.

Example:

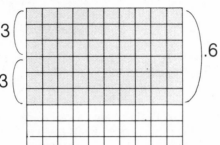

.6 ÷ .3 = _2_

1. .8 ÷ .2 = __

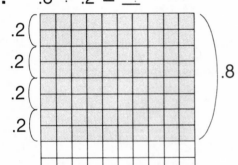

3. .9 ÷ .3 = __

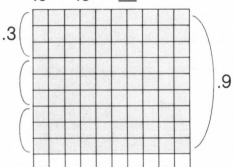

2. 1.0 ÷ .5 = __

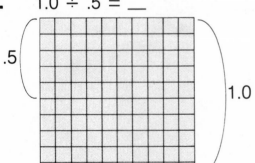

4. .8 ÷ .4 = __

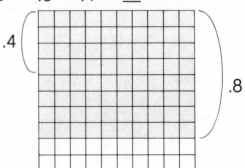

5. 1.0 ÷ .2 = __   **6.** .4 ÷ .2 = __   **7.** 1.4 ÷ .7 = __

8. 2.5 ÷ .5 = __   **9.** 1.5 ÷ .3 = __   **10.** 3.0 ÷ 1.0 = __

•*Materials*   Paper, pencils, Work Sheet 6-E3.

•***Procedure***   Students may now be introduced to a decimal-fraction division algorithm. In order to develop a useable algorithm for dividing decimals,
however, it is necessary to alter the appearance of the problem. (It should be
explained to students that this alteration merely changes the appearance of the
problem, not the substance.)

When the divisor is a whole number, the proper placement of the decimal
point is much easier than when the divisor is a decimal fraction.

$$
\begin{array}{r}
.14 \\
34\overline{)4.76} \\
\underline{3\,4} \\
1\,36 \\
\underline{1\,36} \\
0
\end{array}
$$

Show students that the decimal point in the answer is simply placed above the
decimal point in the dividend, and the whole-number division algorithm is used.

In order to explain the usefulness of this simplification, the teacher must
first demonstrate a technique developed for generating sets of equivalent fractions: by multiplying the numerator and denominator of a fraction by the same
number,

$$\frac{3}{4} \times \frac{10}{10} = \frac{30}{40}$$

you can change the appearance of the fraction without altering the substance
(i.e., $\frac{3}{4} = \frac{30}{40}$). When the divisor in a division problem contains a fraction part, it
is necessary to use this same technique to change it into a whole number.

15.66 ÷ 2.7 = ?

$$\frac{15.66}{2.7} = ? \qquad \frac{15.66}{2.7} \times \frac{10}{10} = \frac{156.7}{27}$$

Point out that the divisor is now a whole number and that

$$\frac{15.66}{2.7} = \frac{156.6}{27}$$

It is now possible to solve the problem utilizing the whole-number division
algorithm.

$$
\begin{array}{r}
5.8 \\
27\overline{)156.6} \\
\underline{135} \\
21\,6 \\
\underline{21\,6} \\
0
\end{array}
$$

Therefore, 15.66 ÷ 2.7 = 5.8.

By observing the changing position of the decimal point, children may recognize a pattern and a means of further simplifying the algorithm. That is, by moving the decimal point of the divisor and the dividend the same number of places (the number of places necessary to make the divisor a whole number) we accomplish the same result as when we use the equivalent-fraction technique.

Example 1.   **4.32 ÷ .18 = 432. ÷ 18.**

$$
\begin{array}{r}
24 \\
18.\overline{)432.} \\
36 \\
\hline
72 \\
72 \\
\hline
0
\end{array}
$$

Example 2.   **55.5 ÷ .15 = 5550. ÷ 15.**

$$
\begin{array}{r}
370 \\
15.\overline{)5550.} \\
45 \\
\hline
105 \\
105 \\
\hline
00 \\
00 \\
\hline
0
\end{array}
$$

Name_____

Move the decimal point to divide by a whole number in each problem.

Examples:

$$2.7\overline{)15.66} \quad = \quad 27.\overline{)156.6}$$
$$\begin{array}{r} 5.8 \\ \hline 135 \\ \hline 216 \\ 216 \\ \hline 0 \end{array}$$

$$.18\overline{)4.32} \quad = \quad 18.\overline{)432.}$$
$$\begin{array}{r} 24. \\ \hline 36 \\ \hline 72 \\ 72 \\ \hline 0 \end{array}$$

1. $.41\overline{)3.17}$

2. $9.6\overline{)15.71}$

3. $13.8\overline{)61.7}$

4. $.06\overline{)7.26}$

5. $2.04\overline{)29.73}$

6. $.61\overline{)8.179}$

7. $9.38\overline{)41.60}$

8 $9.38\overline{)41.6}$

Number Patterns and Functions

Children learning arithmetic commonly see little relationship between the computational processes they are required to memorize and the real world in which they live. Eventually they learn that computation is an excellent tool with which to solve everyday problems. A little more investigation, however, can provide students with a whole new way of looking at the world. Observation of patterns and a thorough understanding of functions will allow them a glimpse of the true power of mathematics.

In the following section, we provide a series of activities that require observation of various physical and symbolic patterns. Each example is summarized by a symbolic function (rule) which describes the situation in the shorthand language of algebra.

Our intent is not to provide a thorough program for familiarization with the notion of function. Consider this section to be a natural extension of the elementary concepts presented in the previous sections—an introduction to the next phase of your students' mathematical development.

Concept A: The Even Numbers

Activity 7-A1.
(concrete)

•*Materials*   Wooden cubes.

•***Procedure***   Have students construct the following pattern with their wooden cubes.

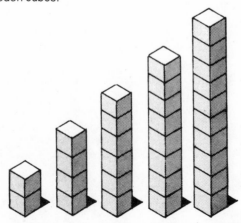

Ask the following sequence of questions in order to introduce the concept of pattern: "How long will the next stack be?"

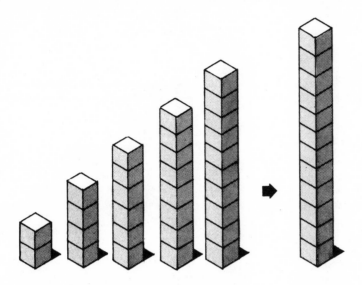

"If I show you any stack, can you show me the next stack in the pattern?"

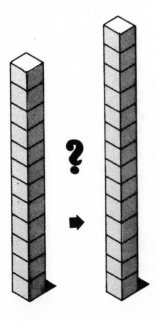

Given any stack, students will find it easy to determine the next stack in the pattern—they simply add two blocks.

Arrange the stacks in the following manner and number them to ease communication.

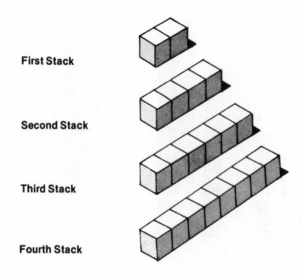

First Stack

Second Stack

Third Stack

Fourth Stack

It is easy to find the fifth stack simply by adding two blocks to the fourth stack.

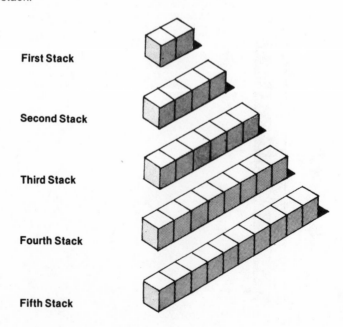

First Stack

Second Stack

Third Stack

Fourth Stack

Fifth Stack

The procedure we used above is called "discovering a pattern." We carefully determine how one stack differs from the one before and with a little faith, assume that the pattern will continue in the same manner forever. Now, by asking one additional question, we discover the difference between a pattern and a function: Observing the same pattern, it is possible to determine what the tenth stack will look like without seeing the ninth stack?

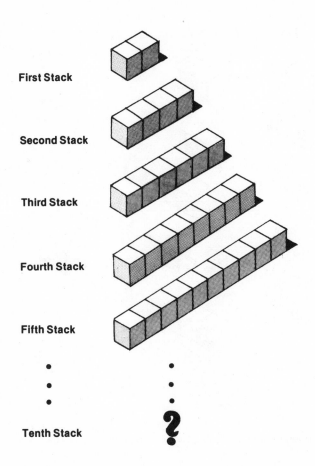

First Stack

Second Stack

Third Stack

Fourth Stack

Fifth Stack

Tenth Stack

In order to solve this problem, students must observe the relationship between the position of a stack (first, second, third, etc.) and the number of blocks in it. For example, in the first stack there are two cubes, in the second stack four cubes, and in the third stack there are six cubes. Show students that if they were to use cubes to denote the relative positions of the stacks, they would have the following pattern:

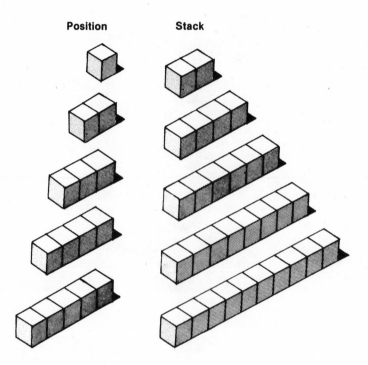

Point out that by doubling the position counters, they will derive the number of cubes in each stack.

Therefore, the solution to the problem is as follows:

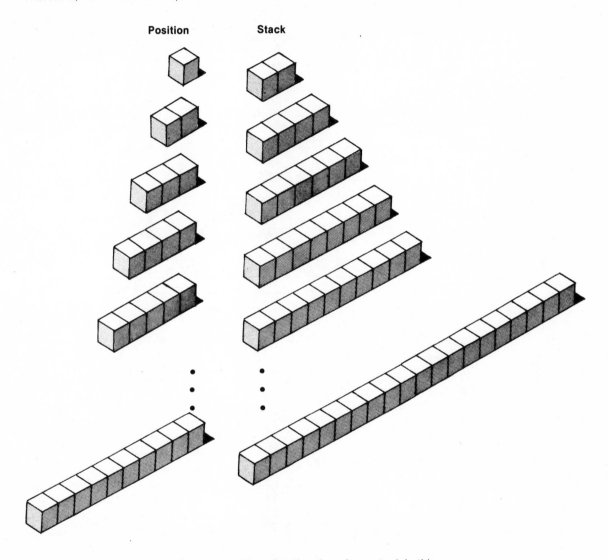

This time-saving procedure allows us to determine the size of any stack in this pattern without having to construct the whole pattern up to that point. It provides us with a great deal of freedom. We call this procedure "discovering a function."

Activity 7-A2.
(representational)

•*Materials*   A supply of one-centimeter (or one-half-inch) graph paper.

•***Procedure***   Follow the same procedure as described in Activity 7-A1. This time, however, have the students draw the pattern on, or cut it out of graph paper. Many students don't require this transition activity, while others may prefer to substitute this exercise for Activity 7-A1.

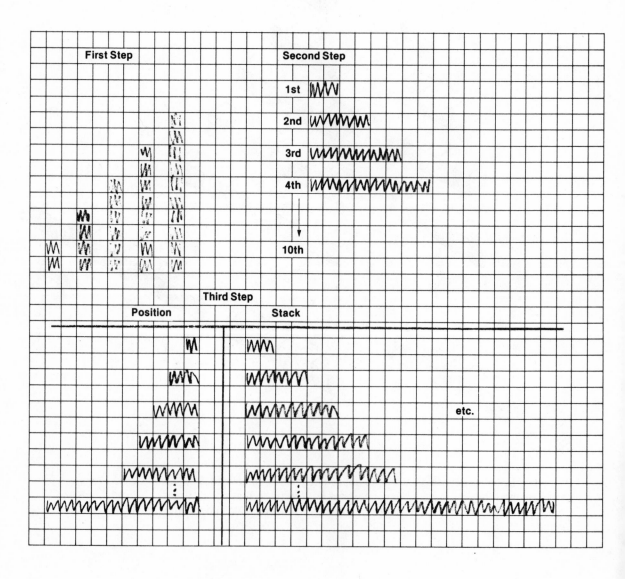

•*Materials*   Paper, pencils, Work Sheet 7-A3.

•***Procedure***   Have each student write the following pattern:

2, 4, 6, 8, 10, 12 . . .

Use the following sequence of questions to establish the concept of number pattern:
   "What number comes next?"

2, 4, 6, 8, 10, 12, 14 . . .

   "If I give you the number 14 from this pattern, can you give me the next number?"

14 ⌒ **16**

Help students see that given any number in this pattern, they can derive the next number by adding two. This procedure, too, is called "discovering a pattern."

   Next, arrange the pattern in the following manner, numbering each position to ease communication.

Position Number	Pattern Number
1	2
2	4
3	6
4	8

In order to determine the tenth number in this pattern, it becomes necessary to discover a function.

Position Number	Pattern Number
1	2
2	4
3	6
4	8
5	10
6	12
.	.
.	.
.	.
10	?

From their experience with the previous activities, students will have learned that doubling the position number gives them the proper answer without their having to generate all the numbers in the pattern.

Position Number	Pattern Number
1	2
2	4
3	6
4	8
5	10
6	12
.	.
.	.
.	.
10	20

This function can be stated in mathematical shorthand as follows:

$2 \times m = n$

where m represents any position number and n represents the corresponding pattern number. For example,

$2 \times 3 = 6$

and $2 \times 5 = 10$

Concept B: The Square Numbers

Activity 7-B1.
(concrete)

•*Materials*   Wooden cubes.

•***Procedure***   Have each student construct the following pattern:

Name_____

Complete the pattern.   Record your results.

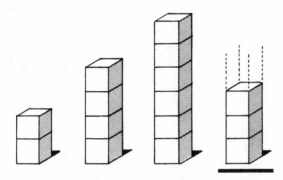

Position Number (*m*)	Pattern Number (*n*)
1	2
2	4
3	6
4	___
5	___
6	___
7	___

How tall is the pile in the tenth position? _____

What rule (function) makes *each* position number into the correct
pattern number? _____

Can you find the rule (function) for this table?

m	*n*
1	1
2	3
3	5
4	7
5	9
6	11
7	13

What is the next stack in this pattern?

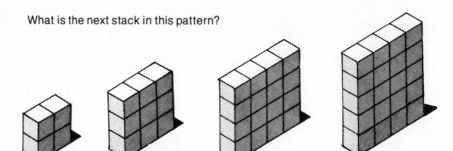

Students will discover that to construct the next stack in this pattern, they need only extend the length and width of the last square by one cube and fill in with more cubes. This procedure is called "discovering a pattern."

It is easier to find the tenth stack in the pattern if one first finds the function. That discovery is facilitated by arranging the stacks in the following manner:

Position   **Stack**

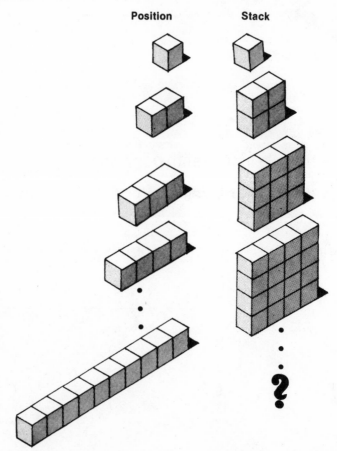

Show students that each pattern stack is formed by building a square with edges as long as the position counters. For example, the third stack is formed by making a square that has three cubes on each edge. (You may remember that this procedure is used in constructing arrays that model multiplication.)

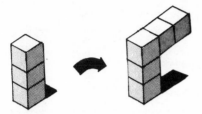

To construct the tenth stack, it is necessary to build a square with ten cubes on each edge. We now have a rule (function) for finding any stack in the pattern.

Position   **Pattern**

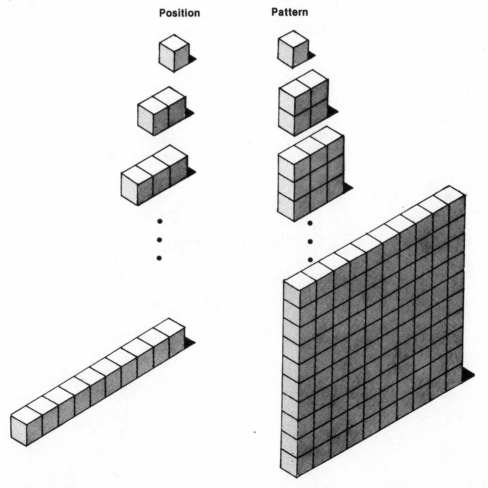

Activity 7-B2.
(representational)

•*Materials*   One-centimeter (or one-half-inch) graph paper.

•***Procedure***   Follow the same procedure as in Activity 7-B1. This time, however, have the students draw the pattern on, or cut it out of, graph paper.

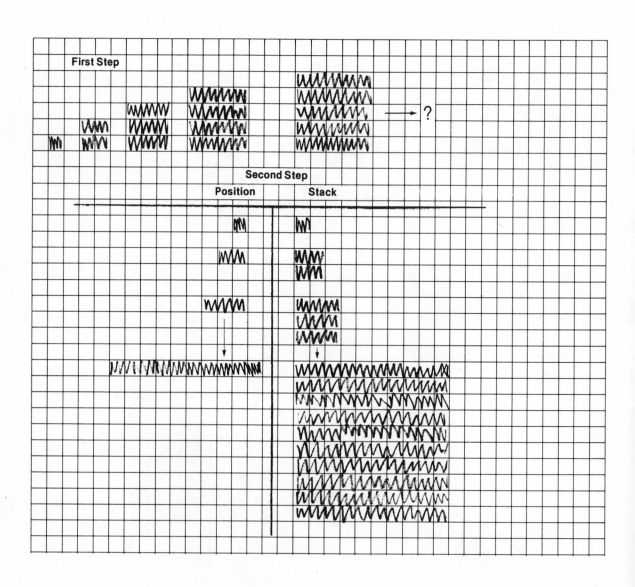

First Step

Second Step

Position   Stack

?

•*Materials* Paper, pencils, Work Sheet 7-B3.

•***Procedure*** Have the students write this pattern:

1, 4, 9, 16 . . .

Ask them what number comes next. (As a hint, tell them to determine the difference between each number pair and observe how the difference "grows.")

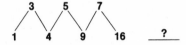

They will learn that to find the next number in the pattern, they must add the next odd number in the difference pattern (nine) to the last number in the sequence (sixteen); i.e., $16 + 9 = 25$. Therefore,

1, 4, 9, 16, 25 . . .

In order to determine the tenth number in this pattern without having to determine, one by one, all the numbers that come before it, we must first find the function for this pattern.

Arrange the pattern in the following manner:

Position Number	Pattern Number
1	1
2	4
3	9
4	16
.	.
.	.
.	.
10	?

From their experience with the previous activities and by remembering the development of arrays when they worked with multiplication, students should notice that the pattern numbers can be generated by multiplying each corresponding number by itself.

Position Number		Pattern Number
2 × 2	=	4
3 × 3	=	9
.		.
.		.
.		.

Hence, the solution to the problem:

Position Number	Pattern Number
1	1
2	4
3	9
4	16
.	.
.	.
.	.
10	100

Writing this function in mathematical shorthand, we have

$m \times m = n$

where m is any position number and n is its corresponding pattern number.

$3 \times 3 = 9$

or $5 \times 5 = 25$

or $21 \times 21 = 441$

Concept C: The Triangle Numbers

Activity 7-C1.
(concrete)

•*Materials*   Wooden cubes.

•***Procedure***   Have each student construct the following pattern:

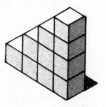

Name_____

Complete the pattern. Record your results.

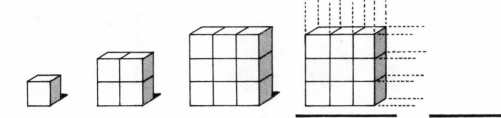

Position Number (m)	Pattern Number (n)
1	1
2	4
3	9
4	___
5	___

How many blocks will be in the ninth pile?_____

What rule (function) makes *each* position number into the correct pattern number? _____

Can you find the rule (function) for this table?

m	n
1	2
2	5
3	10
4	17
5	26
6	37

Ask, "Can you construct the next stack in this pattern?"

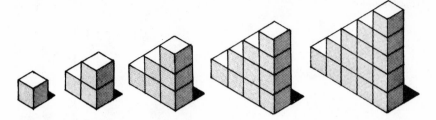

Each new stack can be constructed by building a new set of stairs on the old stack.

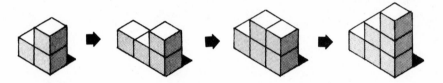

To find the tenth stack, however, students must first find the function for this pattern. Arrange the stacks as follows:

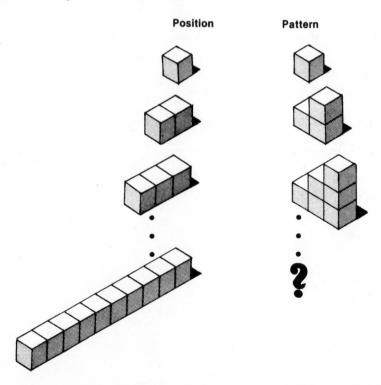

Once it has been discovered that each stack is built by starting with the cor-responding position number and building stairs on top of it, that rule (function) can be used to solve the problem.

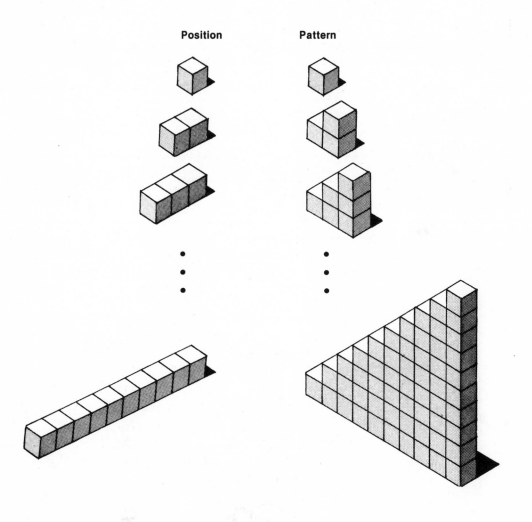

Position   Pattern

Activity 7-C2.
(representational)

•*Materials*   One-centimeter (or one-half-inch) graph paper.

•**Procedure**   Follow the same procedure as for Activity 7-C1, this time having the students draw the patterns on, or cut them out of, graph paper.

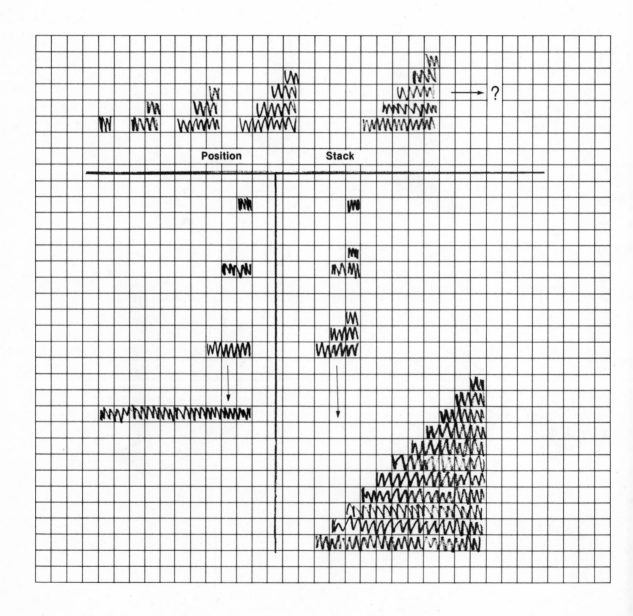

•*Materials*   Paper, pencils, Work Sheet 7-C3.

•*Procedure*   Have each student write the following number pattern:

1, 3, 6, 10 . . .

Ask them what number comes next. (As a hint, tell them to determine the differences between each number pair and observe how the difference "grows.")

They will find that the next difference should be five. To determine the next number in the pattern, then, they need only add the next number in the difference pattern.

1, 3, 6, 10, 15 . . .

To find the tenth number in the pattern, it is first necessary to find the function. Have students arrange the pattern in the following manner:

Position Number	Pattern Number
1	1
2	3
3	6
4	10
.	.
.	.
.	.
10	?

Based on their experiences with previous activities, and noting that when they construct a stack in this manner they are simply adding up natural number sequences,

$$1 + 2 + 3 + 4 + 5 = 15$$

students will see that to find the tenth pattern number, they must add all the natural numbers from one to ten; i.e., $1 + 2 + 3 + 4 + 5 + 6 + 7 + 8 + 9 + 10 = 55$. Therefore, using our rule (function) we have:

Position Number	Pattern Number
1	1
2	3
3	6
4	10
.	.
.	.
.	.
10	55

Since we can write the sum $1 + 2 + 3 + 4 + 5 + 6 + 7 + 8 + 9 + 10 = 55$ as

$$\begin{array}{rrrrr} 1 & 2 & 3 & 4 & 5 \\ + 10 & 9 & 8 & 7 & 6 \\ \hline \end{array}$$
$$11 + 11 + 11 + 11 + 11 = 5 \times 11$$

we can write the function in mathematical shorthand as follows:

$$\frac{m}{2} \times (m + 1) = \frac{m(m + 1)}{2} = n$$

where m is any position number and n is the corresponding pattern number. In this example $\frac{m}{2} = 5$ and $(m + 1) = 11$.

$$(1 + 2 + 3) = \frac{3 \times (3 + 1)}{2} = 6$$

$$\text{or } (1 + 2 + 3 + 4) = \frac{4 \times (4 + 1)}{2} = 10$$

$$\text{or } (1 + 2 + 3 + 4 + \ldots + 50) = \frac{50 \times (50 + 1)}{2} = 1275$$

$$\text{or } (1 + 2 + 3 + 4 + \ldots + 100) = \frac{100 \times (100 + 1)}{2} + 5050$$

Name_____

Complete the pattern.   Record your results.

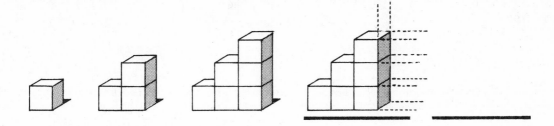

Position Number (m)	Pattern Number (n)
1	1
2	3
3	6
4	___
5	___

How many blocks will be in the seventh pile? _____

What rule (function) makes *each* position number into the correct pattern number? _____

Can you find the rule (function) for this table?

m	n
1	0
2	1
3	3
4	6
5	10
6	15

Concept D: Ten Men in a Boat

Activity 7-D1.
*(concrete/
symbolic)*

•*Materials*   Puzzle board, Work Sheet 7-D1.

Note: There are several puzzles that can be solved using techniques developed in the previous activities. One interesting example is "Ten Men in a Boat."

•**Procedure**   Ten men are in a fishing boat. There are eleven seats in the boat, the middle one empty.

All the fishermen in the stern have red beards and all the fishermen in the bow have black beards. The five men in the back of the boat decide that the fishing is better in the front, and the five in the front decide the fishing is better in back. They all agree to change places. To ensure that the boat will not capsize, they also agree to the following rule: *Any man can move to an empty seat next to him or climb over at most one man into an empty seat on the other side.* What is the minimum number of moves required for all the fishermen in the front of the boat to change places with those in the back?

A practice puzzle of this type can easily be constructed from a small piece of wood and ten golf tees, five red and five black. Drill eleven holes and place the tees in the proper positions.

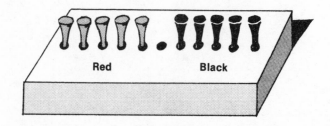

In order to solve this puzzle, we will use the following problem-solving technique: *If you can't solve a difficult problem, make up a simpler problem which is similar to the difficult one. Using the insight gained from the simpler problem, attempt to solve the more complicated one.*

To solve our fishermen problem, let's first see how many moves would be required if there were only one pair of fishermen in the boat.

One Move

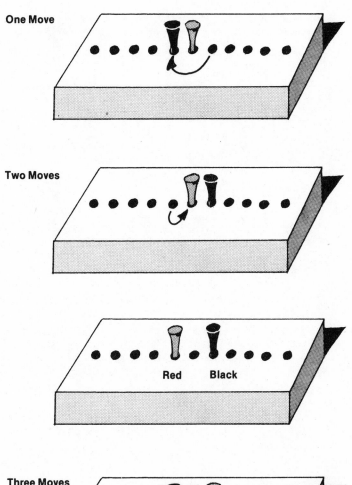

Two Moves

Red   Black

Three Moves

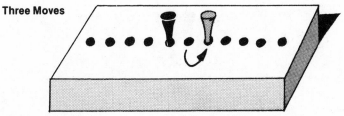

It takes three moves for one pair of fishermen to change places.

Pairs of Fishermen	Minimum Number of Moves
1	3

With two pairs of fishermen, we would make the following moves:

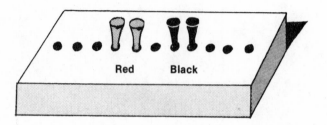

One Move

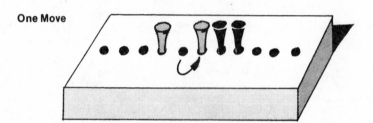

Two Moves

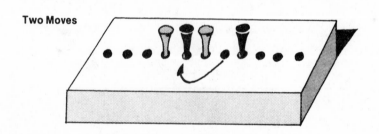

Three Moves

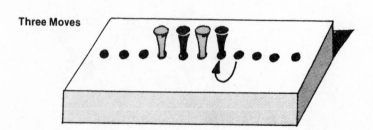

Four Moves

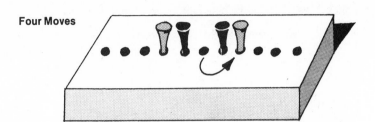

Five Moves

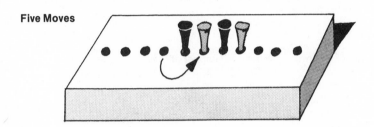

Six Moves

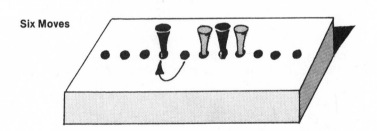

Seven Moves

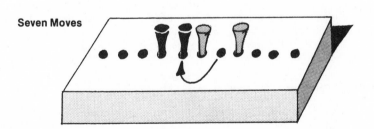

Eight Moves

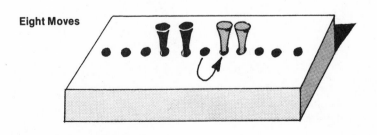

It takes eight moves for two pairs of fishermen to change places.

Pairs of Fishermen	Minimum Number of Moves
1	3
2	8

To exchange three pairs of fishermen requires fifteen moves. And for four pairs, it takes twenty-four moves. The reader can verify the above statements with his puzzle board.

Pairs of Fishermen	Minimum Number of Moves
1	3
2	8
3	15
4	24
5	?

To determine the minimum number of moves for five pairs, we can examine the differences between number pairs in the pattern and observe how they "grow."

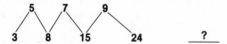

The differences form a pattern of odd numbers. Adding the next odd number, 11, to 24 will solve the problem. Once again, we have used the notion of pattern to find a solution. Our fishermen can change places in 35 moves.

Pairs of Fishermen	Minimum Number of Moves
1	3
2	8
3	15
4	24
5	35

What is the minimum number of moves required to exchange ten pairs of fishermen? To efficiently solve this problem, students must first derive the function for this pattern.

An examination of the table below shows the problem to be one of establishing some rule (function) that will change the first number (pairs of fishermen) into the second number (minimum number of moves) for every number pair in the table. This rule (function) involves some combination of addition, subtraction, multiplication, and/or division. Initially the rule (function) is found by trial-and-error methods. Later the very powerful methods of finite differences may be utilized.[1]

Pairs of Fishermen	Minimum Number of Moves
1	3
2	8
3	15
4	24
5	35
.	.
.	.
10	?

Utilizing trial and error, the student may discover that if the first number (pairs of fishermen) is multiplied by a number two larger than itself, the answer is always the correct number of moves.

$2 \times 4 = 8$

or $4 \times 6 = 24$

or $5 \times 7 = 35$

Students will come up with several rules that work for one or two pairs, but this is the simplest rule (function) that works for *all* cases. Therefore, the solution to the problem is $10 \times 12 = 120$.

Pairs of Fishermen	Minimum Number of Moves
1	3
2	8
3	15
4	24
5	35
.	.
.	.
.	.
10	120

[1] Seymour, Dale and Margaret Shedd, *Finite Differences: A Pattern Discovery Approach to Problem Solving.* Palo Alto, Calif.: Creative Publications, 1973.

Writing the function in mathematical shorthand, we have

$m \times (m + 2) = n$

where m is the number of pairs of fishermen and n is the minimum number of moves.

$5 \times (5 + 2) = 35$

or $10 \times (10 + 2) = 120$

or $50 \times (50 + 2) = 2600$

Functions are among the most powerful tools that mathematics provide. Once students have a thorough understanding of function and its uses, they will find it much easier to think about grappling with some of the very complicated situations with which they are confronted in life. The study of patterns and functions seems to be a natural extension of the study of basic arithmetic. Allow your students a glimpse of the world through the eyes of mathematics, and let them feel the sense of power and satisfaction that can be derived from its use.

Name_____

Record the results of your "Ten Men in a Boat" experiment on this table.

Pairs of Fishermen (m)	Minimum Number of Moves (n)
1 (pair)	3
2	___
3	___
4	___
5	___

What is the minimum number of moves (n) it would take for ten pairs of fishermen (m) to trade places?

_____

What rule (function) makes *each m* into the correct *n*?

_____

Can you find the rule (function) for this table?

m	n
1	0
2	2
3	6
4	12
5	20
6	30

APPENDICES

I. **Hierarchy of Developmental Concepts**
II. **Diagnostic Developmental Activities**
III. **Manipulative Instructional Materials**
IV. **Topic Checklist**

Hierarchy of Developmental Concepts

Cognitive Operation	Until children are competent with respect to each cognitive operation, they should not be expected to:
1. Logical Classification	1. Assign numerals to concrete sets 2. Distinguish attributes of physical objects
2. Seriation	1. Compare sizes of sets 2. Compare numbers ($>$, $<$) 3. Compare lengths 4. Assign numerals to concrete sets
3. Conservation of Number	1. Determine equivalence of sets 2. Compare sizes of sets 3. Assign numerals to concrete sets

The child's effective understanding of the concepts listed above is prerequisite to systematic work with symbolic definition or comparison of whole numbers.

4. Set Inclusion	1. Work with the operations of addition or subtraction symbolically 2. Work with number sentences (missing addends)
5. Transitivity	1. Work with the operations of multiplication or division symbolically 2. Compare the sizes of two objects with a measuring instrument
6. Conservation of Area	1. Define fractional parts by partitioning a whole unit 2. Utilize concrete materials that use area (i.e., geoboards, graph paper) to model abstract mathematical concepts

7. Conservation of Length	1. Use the number line to model number operations
	2. Utilize concrete materials that use length (i.e., Cuisenaire rods, ruler, slide rule) to model abstract mathematical concepts
8. Conservation of Mass	1. Define fractional parts based on a mass model (i.e., use a pan balance to define fractional parts)
	2. Utilize concrete materials that use mass to model abstract mathematical concepts (i.e., Invicta balance, pan balance)

Diagnostic Developmental Activities

In order to achieve any meaningful understanding of numbers and operations, the student must possess certain prerequisite intellectual capabilities. The eight cognitive operations listed in Appendix I can be grouped into two categories: (1) those dealing with conservation (invariance) and (2) those dealing with classification.

The following activities provide a means of diagnosing whether a child has developed sufficient competence relative to each intellectual skill. The activities should be presented to each child in one-to-one interview situations. The results of the interview and the suggestions provided in Appendix I should assist you in placing each student in the proper activity level.[1]

Note that a student must deal effectively with logical classification, seriation, and conservation of number in order to define and compare numbers. Students who do not meet these criteria should be encouraged to experience many concrete and representational activities, since activities at the symbolic level will be of little benefit. Children develop competence with these three cognitive operations at about the same time—i.e., at six or seven years of age. Some children, however, achieve these intellectual capabilities a little earlier, and some much later.

Students who do not deal effectively with set inclusion are not intellectually prepared to work with the operations of addition and subtraction. Rarely do children achieve this concept before seven years of age. This implies that formal addition and subtraction instruction, especially at the symbolic level, should be started at about the second grade. First-grade students might then have a greater opportunity to experience concrete and representational activities.

Once students are dealing effectively with transitivity, instruction in multiplication can begin. Interestingly enough, understanding of transitivity is also achieved at about age seven. This suggests that instruction in addition should begin a little later and multiplication a little earlier than scheduled in the curricula utilized by most districts in the United States.

Competence with conservation of area, length, and mass should be assessed prior to addressing such concepts in measurement activities or utilizing measurement models which provide a basis for more complex mathematical concepts, such as fractions, decimals, and various aspects of geometry.

---

[1]For detailed discussion see Richard W. Copeland, *How Children Learn Mathematics (New York: McMillan, 1974).*

Logical Classification

(Number Readiness)   •*Purpose:*   This activity evaluates a student's ability to sort (classify) objects consistently based on observable likenesses and differences.

•*Materials:*   A set of shapes similar to those below. Each shape should be provided in two colors.

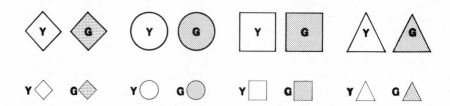

•**Procedure:**   Have the student dump the blocks onto the table and ask him to sort them into two groups so that each group is alike in some way. Children who do not classify logically will have difficulty with this problem. They may change their grouping criteria in the middle of the problem or may simply make pretty patterns with the shapes. In most cases, children between the ages of two and six fall into this category. Around age six, children generally become more adept at solving this problem but nevertheless require some help with organization in order to ensure that all the blocks will fit into one group or the other. Between the ages of six and eight, most children are able to solve this problem independently and without hesitation, providing complete descriptions of their grouping criteria.

Until a child can classify logically, it is not advisable to introduce number concepts at the abstract level. Number concepts should remain implicit in the concrete materials and not formally defined by means of symbols.

Seriation

(Number Readiness)   •*Purpose:*   This activity evaluates a student's ability to place objects in serial order based on some attribute of size.

•*Materials:*   Ten paper cutouts of workers gradually increasing in size, with the largest twice as big as the smallest. In addition, you will need ten paper cutouts of shovels gradually increasing in size, with the largest three times as big as the smallest.

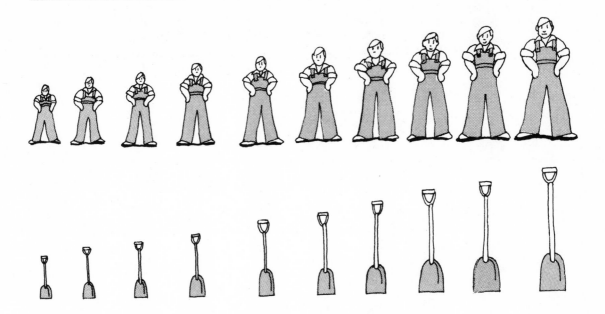

•**Procedure:** Ask the child to arrange the workers in order from small to large. Then have him position the shovels so that each worker gets the right-size shovel. Mix the workers up and ask the child to rearrange the shovels accordingly. Next give him the shovels, point to one of the workers, and ask the child to produce the appropriate shovel.

Young children (two to five years old) are unable to seriate either the workers or the shovels. Over the next two years, most children develop the ability to solve the three seriation problems, primarily by trial-and-error methods. Generally abilities necessary to solve the three problems are acquired in the order in which the problems have been listed above. After age six, most children readily solve all three seriation problems without using trial and error.

Until a child can deal effectively with concrete seriation problems, number concepts should not be introduced at the abstract (symbolic) level. Seriation is very closely tied to the concepts of cardinal and ordinal numbers and should therefore be prerequisite to the formal introduction of these concepts.

Conservation of Number

•*Purpose:* This activity evaluates a student's understanding of the invariance (conservation) of the number of objects in a set when the elements are moved about.

(Number Readiness)

•*Materials:* Twelve identical wooden cubes.

•**Procedure:** Make a row of six cubes in front of you. Give the rest of the cubes to the child and ask him if he has the same number of cubes as you have. Have him prove it by putting the blocks in one-to-one correspondence, as below.

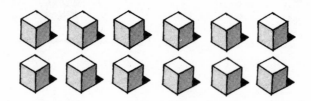

Now spread his blocks out and ask him whether you both still have the same amount.

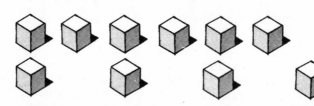

Young children (four to five years of age) have difficulty determining whether the numbers of blocks are equal and generally cannot place the two sets in one-to-one correspondence in the first place. Even if they can initially determine equivilence by putting the two sets into one-to-one correspondence, when the rows are transformed their decisions are ruled by perceptual considerations; therefore, they believe that the spread-out row contains more cubes. Over the next two years, they will become capable of putting the blocks in one-to-one correspondence, but the decisions will still be ruled by perceptual appearances. By the age of seven, children are usually able to solve this problem correctly. We then say that the child conserves number.

As with classification and seriation, it is not recommended that children be introduced to number concepts at the abstract level until they conserve number. Once children are dealing effectively with classification, seriation, and conservation of number, they are ready to be introduced to the abstract notion of number and the associated symbols.

Set Inclusion

(Addition and Subtraction Readiness)   •*Purpose:*   This activity evaluates a student's understanding of the concept of a whole in relation to its parts.

•*Materials:*   Two kinds of flowers (e.g., daisies and carnations)—seven of one (daisies) and three of the other (carnations).

•***Procedure:***   Ask the child whether the daisies are flowers and whether the carnations are flowers. Then ask, "If you were to make bouquets, which would be larger, the bouquet of daisies or the bouquet of flowers?" Children under seven will generally indicate that the bouquet of daisies would be larger. They cannot simultaneously consider the *whole* set of flowers and at the same time distinguish between the *parts* (daisies and carnations). The child who is unable to deal with set inclusion is unable to reverse the process by breaking up a whole and realizing that a recombination of the parts is once again equivalant to the whole. This is analogous to a child's knowing that $3 + 5 = 8$ but not recognizing that $8 = 3 + 5$. Around the age of seven, children are able to consider both the whole and its parts simultaneously and can therefore solve the set-inclusion problem.

Before children have acquired a thorough understanding of set inclusion, it is not advisable to introduce the operation of addition and subtraction at the formal (symbolic) level. When addition is introduced before a child has gained competence with set inclusion, any learning may be rote in nature and true understanding of the concept may be delayed.

Transitivity

•*Purpose:*   This activity evaluates a student's ability to recognize the equivalence of sets in an array rather than depending on one-to-one correspondence or counting methods to make that determination.

(Multiplication Readiness)

•*Materials:*   Ten daisies, ten carnations, and ten vases.

•***Procedure:***   Have the child put one daisy in each vase. Remove the daisies and repeat the procedure with the carnations. Ask whether he has used the same number of daisies as carnations. Then ask, "If all the flowers were put back in vases in the same manner as before, how many flowers would be in each vase?"

Children under six years old are generally unable to answer either question correctly. They are unable to conserve number, so when the daisies are removed and replaced by the carnations, they must re-count or place them in one-to-one correspondence in order to justify equality. These children are also unable to use the transitive property to assist them in solving the problem. That property could be described as follows:

Number of Daisies = Number of Vases

Number of Carnations = Number of Vases

Number of Daisies = Number of Carnations

Between six and seven years of age, however, children generally solve both problems readily, providing correct responses to the second question even when three, four, or more sets of flowers are considered.

Competence with the transitive property is of primary importance in the learning of multiplication skills. Transitivity and set-inclusion concepts develop in children at approximately the same time. This implies that while in the mathematics programs presently in use addition may be introduced a year early, introduction of multiplication may take place a year late! In any case, systematic introduction of symbolic multiplication should be delayed until after competence with transitivity is attained.

Conservation of Area

(Fraction Readiness)

•*Purpose:*   This activity evaluates a student's understanding of the invariance of a concrete object's area when the object is divided into pieces.

•*Materials:*   Two equal cardboard rectangles, one cut diagonally to form two equal triangles.

•***Procedure:***   Place the two triangles on the rectangle so that the triangles fit the surface of the rectangle. Once the child has agreed that these areas are equal (i.e. that the same amount of paint would be required to cover the triangles as to cover the rectangle) remove the triangles and arrange them as below.

  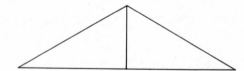

Ask the child whether the two shapes are still the same size (i.e., whether they would require the same amount of paint to cover them). Most children under the age of seven will say that the second figure is larger. They are guided by their perception: the second figure has more pieces or simply appears larger. Between the ages of seven and eight, most children develop the notion that cutting and moving the pieces about does not change the total area. They are able to mentally reverse the procedure in order to justify their conclusions. Since the definition of fraction is often based on the area concept, formal work with fractions should be delayed until after understanding of area conservation is developed. Introducing informal investigations with fractional parts and fractional parts of sets of objects is appropriate only if conservation-of-number concepts have been mastered.

Conservation of Length

•*Purpose:* This activity will help the teacher evaluate a student's understanding of the invariance (conservation) of the linear qualities of concrete objects when they are moved about.

•*Materials:* Two equally long pieces of heavy cord.

•***Procedure:*** Present the following situation to the child: If two equally fast crawly-bugs were put on the end of these strings

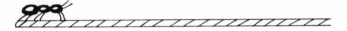

and they both went the same speed, would they reach the end at the same time? How about these two strings? (Use the same strings.)

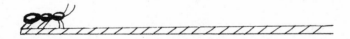

And these? (Again, use the same strings.)

Most children under six years old will not realize that the race would be a tie in the second and third cases even though they know you are using the same string. Around the age of six or seven, most children conserve length and give the correct response because they are able to reverse the process, mentally moving the strings into their original positions.

Children who do not conserve length should not be expected to measure with a ruler, since when they move the ruler it seems to get longer! The number line is of no help to a nonconserver of length. That child perceives the distance between four and five on the number line as being greater than the distance between one and two. Other, more perceptually sound models should be used in such cases.

Conservation of Mass

•*Purpose:*   This activity serves to evaluate a student's understanding of the invariance of the mass of a concrete object when its shape is transformed.

•*Materials:*   Two equal amounts of clay.

•***Procedure:***   Have the child hold the two pieces of clay and transfer clay from one to the other until both pieces are equal. Roll each piece into a ball and place them on the table in front of the student. Then roll one ball into a long sausage, leaving the other untouched. Ask the child whether both pieces are still the "same amount." Before age eight, most children will answer that the amount of clay has changed. Around the age of nine, however, most children are able to reverse the transformation mentally and to conclude that, since no clay was added or taken away, the mass has remained the same.

The introduction of mass-measurement concepts at the symbolic level to nonconservers of mass is not recommended. Furthermore, models such as the balance, which utilizes the mass concept to define number operations, should be avoided until mass conservation is attained. Considerable concrete experience with such devices, however, will optimize instruction at the primary level.

Manipulative Instructional Materials

Various concrete materials may be utilized in the teaching of any specific concept outlined in Topics 1–7. Inexpensive and readily available materials were recommended wherever possible. Substitutions can be made for the suggested materials whenever appropriate and available. For example, older children find tile strips more appropriate than bean sticks for experimenting with place value and number operations. Commercial materials such as Cuisenaire rods, squares, and cubes; or base-ten blocks may be substituted for tile strips and bean sticks.

Brief descriptions of the teaching aids recommended in this book (with suggested alternatives) are provided below.

Attribute Blocks.

Attribute blocks are commercial materials consisting of a set of thirty-two blocks in four different colors (red, blue, yellow, and green), four different shapes (circle, square, diamond, and triangle), and two sizes (big and little). They are used in number-recognition and early classification activities (Topic 1). Some sets come with cards, loops, and problems concerning set inclusion and attribute discrimination. They are available from Creative Publications, Incorporated.

Alternative Materials:

Asco Blocks—Creative Publications, Inc.

Pattern Blocks—Creative Publications, Inc.

Dyed Macaroni

Base-Ten Blocks.

Base-ten blocks are commercially available wooden blocks that utilize a volume model to represent units, tens, hundreds, and thousands place values.

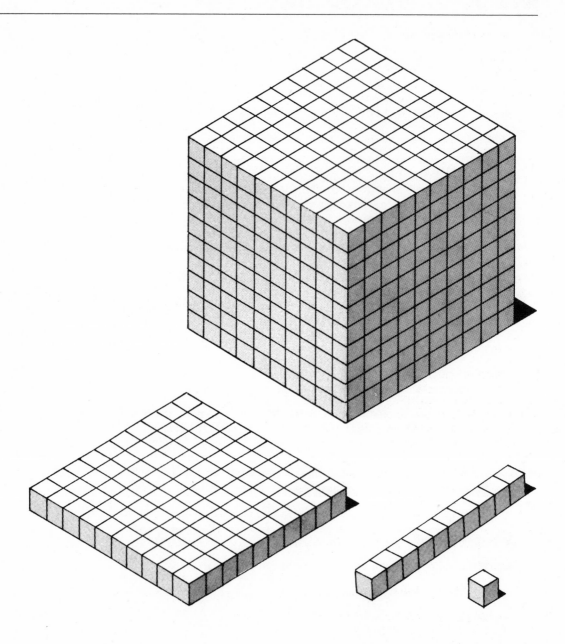

Each unit cube is etched in the surface of each larger block. These blocks provide excellent models for place-value and number-operation activities (Topics 2, 3, 4, 6). They are available from Creative Publications Inc.

Alternative Materials:

Bean Sticks

Tile Strips

Number Blox—Creative Publications Inc.

Cuisenaire Rods, Squares, and Cubes—Cuisenaire Company of America

Bean Sticks.

Bean sticks are student-constructed materials used primarily for number-operations activities. They are created by gluing exactly ten dried pinto beans on a tongue depressor. Ten sticks can be glued together into a raft of 100 beans for work with larger place values. Each child should make a quantity of sticks and rafts. These along with a few loose beans constitute an appropriate concrete system for modeling place value and computation algorithms (Topics 2, 3, 4). Bean sticks are especially appropriate for use by young children.

Alternative Materials:

Base-Ten Blocks—Creative Publications Inc.

Number Blox—Creative Publications Inc.

Cuisenaire Rods, Squares, and Cubes—Cuisenaire Company of America

Cuisenaire Rods.

Cuisenaire rods are commercially available proportioned wooden rods of various colors. They can be used to provide a linear model for whole- and fractional-number operations (Topics 2, 3, 4, and 5). Available from Cuisenaire Company of America.

Alternative Materials:

Unifix Cubes—Creative Publications Inc.

Fraction Tiles.

Fraction tiles are homemade materials consisting of seven congruent squares of different colors, each cut into a different number of equal pieces.

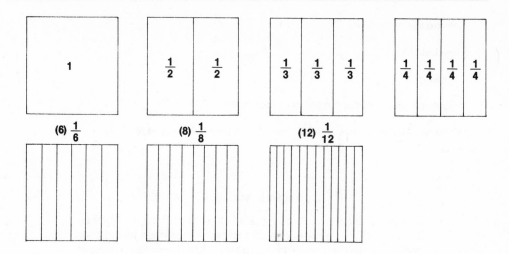

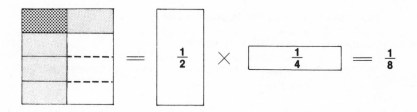

The tiles are used in activities involving addition, subtraction, and multiplication of fractions (Topic 5). To best illustrate fraction multiplication, the tiles should be made of translucent plastic so that the product will be clearly visible.

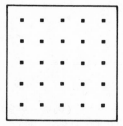

Geoboards.

Geoboards can be constructed by cutting a sheet of half-inch plywood into ten-inch squares. A grid is constructed, consisting of five rows of five nails, two inches apart, that begin one inch from the edge of the board.

The geoboard has many uses, chief of which is its use as an area model for fractional-number operation (Topic 5). Geoboards are also available commercially, from Creative Publications Inc.

Alternative Materials:

Tangrams—Creative Publications Inc.

Discovery Blocks—Creative Publications Inc.

Pattern Blocks—Creative Publication Inc.

Tile Strips.

Tile strips are student-constructed materials used primarily for number-operation activities. Tile strips are formed by gluing exactly ten small bathroom-type ceramic tiles onto strips of heavy cardboard. Ten-by-ten arrays of tiles are also glued to squares of heavy cardboard for work with larger place values. Small, one-centimeter-square tiles are the handiest to use, though one-inch-square tiles work well and are easier to find. Large tile outlets generally have cases of old off-color tiles which they will sell cheaply. While older children may consider bean sticks inappropriate for their age level, they will readily use tile strips as concrete area models for advanced algorithms (Topics 2, 3, 4).

Alternative Materials:

Base-Ten Blocks—Creative Publications Inc.

Number Blox—Creative Publications Inc.

Cuisenaire Rods, Squares, and Cubes—Cuisenaire Company of America

Unifix Cubes.

Unifix cubes are small interlocking plastic cubes of various colors. They are very useful in providing a linear model for elementary number recognition and addition/subtraction operations (Topics 1 and 2). Unifix cubes are especially effective in teaching young children and are the only commercial material we find absolutely essential for primary mathematics instruction. They too are available from Creative Publications Inc.

Alternative Materials:

Cuisenaire Rods—Cuisenaire Company of America

Topic Checklist

Topic: Addition & Subtraction

Concept		Activities		Students →
A	Place Value	1 Concrete / 2 Representational / 3 Symbolic		
B	Place Value	1 Concrete / 2 Representational / 3 Symbolic		
C	Addition of Small Numbers	1 Concrete / 2 Representational / 3 Symbolic		
D	Subtraction of Small Numbers	1 Concrete / 2 Representational / 3 Symbolic		
E	Addition Facts	1 Concrete / 2 Representational / 3 Symbolic		
F	Subtraction Facts	1 Concrete / 2 Representational / 3 Symbolic		
G	Two-digit Addition	1 Concrete / 2 Representational / 3 Symbolic		
H	Two-digit Subtraction	1 Concrete / 2 Representational / 3 Symbolic		

Student columns (each with S = start, F = finish):

1. David Thile
2. Daniel Dodgen
3. Heidi Janzen
4. Grace Zimmerman
5. Chris Halkin
6. Brenda Carter
7.–16. (blank)

The grid cells contain handwritten start/finish dates (e.g. 10/5, 10/10, 10/15, 10/20, 10/25, 10/30) recording each student's progress through the concepts and activities.

Instructional notes:

Dates are recorded when students start (S) and finish (F) each activity. If activity is completed in one day, that date is recorded with a line: 10/1 —

Sometimes students may skip the representational stage of an activity; this can also be seen on the chart.

This chart is provided for your convenience as a detailed recording system. It is not a necessary part of the program.

Teachers fill in the topic and concepts being covered on each recording sheet. Two sheets will be needed for an entire class record.

EXAMPLE COPY

Concept	Activities	Topic: 1	2	3	4	5	6	7	8	9	10	11	12	13	14	15	16
A	1 Concrete / 2 Representational / 3 Symbolic	S F	S F	S F	S F	S F	S F	S F	S F	S F	S F	S F	S F	S F	S F	S F	S F
B	1 Concrete / 2 Representational / 3 Symbolic																
C	1 Concrete / 2 Representational / 3 Symbolic																
D	1 Concrete / 2 Representational / 3 Symbolic																
E	1 Concrete / 2 Representational / 3 Symbolic																
F	1 Concrete / 2 Representational / 3 Symbolic																
G	1 Concrete / 2 Representational / 3 Symbolic																
H	1 Concrete / 2 Representational / 3 Symbolic																

Index